House of Shadows

JANELLE PARSONS
PUBLISHING

House of Shadows is a powerful insight into the devastating impact of generational abuse and the strength that can be found from within to do the inner work and overcome tragedy. This is a truly inspiring story of how one woman overcame the horrors of abuse to live a happy and joyful life. Love doesn't hurt is the powerful theme of this text and should be communicated to all, young and old alike.
Dr Karen Sutherland, Senior Lecturer, University of the Sunshine Coast, Co-Founder - Dharana Digital.

The author opens up about her life and the abuse that she has endured. Easy to read yet compelling life story of how one woman dealt with domestic violence both as a child and adult. The love of her children and the need to protect them gave her courage and strength to escape her shadows. I love this quote: 'Forgive yourself. Love yourself. Be proud that you have the power and ability within you to escape your house of shadows'.
Anonymous Reader and victim of abuse.

House Of Shadows is a compelling, powerful, raw insight into a woman's journey from childhood to adulthood. The life experiences and traumatic events that Janelle reveals will have you on the edge wanting to know more with every single turn of the page. This book reminds you that you are certainly not alone. You will not only feel inspired, but also feel hope, guidance and power to heal and over come those shadows you also face.
Chloe.

A POWERFUL, INSPIRING MEMOIR
OF ONE WOMAN'S JOURNEY TO SET HERSELF FREE
FROM GENERATIONAL ABUSE

House of Shadows

Janelle Parsons

©2022 Janelle Parsons

All Rights reserved.
This book is subject to international copyright law.
No part can be reproduced without express permission
from the author.

www.janelleparsons.com

Cover Art by Janelle Parsons
Cover Design by Aishah Macgill
Typesetting by Aishah Macgill
www.finitepublishing.com

ISBN 978-0-646-85466-3

Trigger Warning:
This book contains sensitive matter relating to domestic violence and sexual abuse. Please also note that some names have been changed.

Categories: Non-Fiction, Biography.

JANELLE PARSONS
PUBLISHING

Dedication

For my children, Maddie and Jayden.
Thank you for being my shining light.

To you, the reader,
thank you for choosing to stand in your own truth.

Contents

Chapter 1	The House of Shadows	1
Chapter 2	A Line Is Crossed	7
Chapter 3	Darkness Descends	15
Chapter 4	Misdirected Anger	25
Chapter 5	A Painful Loss	31
Chapter 6	An Escape	41
Chapter 7	Lured Back In	55
Chapter 8	A Change of Scenery	65
Chapter 9	A Mother's Battle	75
Chapter 10	Cutting Ties	89
Chapter 11	Out Of The Blue	103
Chapter 12	The Twin Flame	121
Chapter 13	A Hint of Deception	129
Chapter 14	Torn	137
Chapter 15	Uncertainty Creeps In	149
Chapter 16	The Rescue Mission	161
Chapter 17	Tethered	173
Chapter 18	The Point of No Return	181
Chapter 19	My Own House of Shadows	191
Chapter 20	Reaching Within	201
Chapter 21	Saving Me	207
	Acknowledgements	215
	About the Author	217

Chapter 1

The House of Shadows

My heart is racing, not from an innocent game of tag with my sisters, but from the terror and uncertainty of what will happen in the next few minutes. His growling voice took on an even scarier sound and even though it is not my fault, I know my father is transforming into a complete stranger.

◊

I may only be six years old, but I am already wise enough to know there is nothing I can do. He is so tall and strong, but instead of making me feel safe, they are traits I fear. I have to bide my time and ride this out until the anger leaves his body and he tires of battering mine. Lost inside myself, I learned to survive by closing my eyes and taking myself to a magical place, away from the physical pain of the incessant licks of the thick leather belt, or the force of a grown man's hand hitting me until my skin was littered with welts.

Every time this happened, another piece of my heart broke.

My younger sisters, Alice and Emily, were even more fragile than me and could not do anything to help. My mother, for reasons I will never understand, refused to. I vividly remember the echo of my siblings begging my father to stop while my mother, who was meant to be my protector, stood helpless and frozen by what was unfolding before her.

One of the first lessons my father taught me was that pain equals love.

Why did this happen? Did I do something wrong? I never received any explanation for the beatings, even when I spent hours curled up in my room crying, willing the darkness to go away and for the pain to stop. Before those beatings began, shortly after I started primary school, I played happily from sunrise to sunset with my classmates and then my two younger sisters. My big blue eyes were filled with joy and my mind danced with images conjured up by my limitless imagination.

But from the moment my father struck me for the first time, another version of myself began to emerge – a girl who was frail and weak, terrified of life and scarred by the memories that were replacing those created in carefree days.

◊

On the outside, my childhood was an idyllic one. Growing up in the bush in a cookie-cutter family home on Epsilon Avenue in Sunset, Queensland, there was so much beauty around our house. I used to love escaping into the backyard to climb trees. But as the shadows grew larger inside our home, my favourite tree in the backyard transformed from a place of happiness to a refuge of safety.

With no support within the walls of my home and a blood-chilling fear drilled into me of the consequences if I were ever to dare speak of the horrors I endured at home to anyone else, the shadows within my mind also grew at a pace I had no control over. In many ways, I had taken on the responsibility of the protector of all of the women in my house – even my mother. I figured if he was distracted by beating me, they would remain untouched.

Looking back, it was far too much for a child to take on, yet whenever there was any glimmer of hope that I had an opportunity to unburden myself and speak up, my mind would buzz with: *Who can you trust? What will happen if he finds out you've told someone? Will he hurt my sisters next? Will he hurt Mum?* These thoughts played with me, controlled me and tricked me. You see, fear is a funny thing and it can drive you to do many things you wouldn't consider normal when looking from the outside in.

As an adult, I understand the power and strength that fear can bring, but as a child it planted the roots of my tree of knowledge – it influenced what I grew up believing. These things were primarily a lack of self-worth, crippling anxiety, fear of failure and a firm belief that my voice doesn't matter. *Just suffer in silence because who would believe you? You're just a child. You must be so naughty to make him mad all the time. You're a liar, it can't be happening.*

This is the sad truth of being raised in a house of shadows.

When I started school, I was so frightened I would run out of the school gates after my mother just begging her to take me away. Other times, I would cling to her legs and have to be peeled off her by a teacher. This didn't go unnoticed by the other kids – I would get teased and called names like cry-baby and sook. Some kids would await my morning arrival so they could point and laugh as it unfolded. The behaviour seemed natural at the time, and with the power of hindsight, I can say that school wasn't really that bad. I was just a frightened child who wanted my mother to notice me, see my pain and take it away for me.

But instead of seeing my desperation, she would firmly grab my hand and say, 'Janelle stop this! You are going to school and everyone is going to look at you now like you are silly.' If there was no teacher on hand to take me calmly, my mother would drag me back into my classroom. I would then sit crossed-legged, shaking and trying my best to stop crying.

With so many insecurities ingrained in me from my traumatic home life, lower primary school was a challenge. I was so worried about failing subjects and failing to make friends that I became the ultimate people pleaser. I thought if I could just make everyone happy, I'd be safe. I'd trade my lunch with the bigger kids so they would leave me alone and would do just about anything anyone told me to. It could be harmless things, like running between two groups in the playground, delivering silly messages. Other times, it could get more serious, like taking the blame for the actions of others and outing myself in uncomfortable situations with people to keep the peace.

My grandparents ran a shelter for Indigenous women and children and they were changing lives in their unique way. Many of the kids at school called me *little white gin* in recognition of the support their families received from my grandparents. It was their way of showing me I was one of them and was very much a term of endearment that was uniquely mine.

◊

As the years rolled by, my school life continued without incident, while the severity of the beatings I was receiving at home only intensified. I would relish the opportunity to get on my bike each weekday morning and feel the soft wind blowing through my hair as I rode to school. This was the quiet time that no one could take away. The distance I put between myself and the house that was simultaneously my place of safety and a place of unspeakable horror was cathartic. Like a snake shedding its skin, the more I pedalled, the more relaxed I became.

Chapter 2

A Line Is Crossed

I hated change and resisted any form of it. But I was especially triggered by changes in my environment. It had become an inbuilt part of me to always seek out the most appropriate safe place anywhere I was.

A change in environment meant my safe place would be compromised. I'd have to find a new one and the pressure of doing that quickly and efficiently led to anxiety. One of the earliest memories I have of this coming to the fore was when I reached Grade 4.

I positively adored my Grade 4 teacher. Her name was Mrs Santillan. She had the longest jet-black hair I've ever seen. She would wrap it around and around on the top of her head, like a crown she dearly loved. When it was out, it would lay on the floor around her feet as she sat at the front of the classroom. Mrs Santillan exuded a quiet strength and was very strict, setting clear boundaries for her classroom while still being a beautiful and kind teacher. I always knew where the line was in her classroom and because I knew and understood the rules, I felt supported. My education blossomed with the structure she provided.

It was the middle of winter and my fingers were chilled to the bone as I walked into my classroom, which had become my safe haven. Mrs Santillan was not in her usual position behind her desk. Panic immediately gripped my chest as I saw an extremely overweight man with a stern expression etched into his ruddy face. The emotions rolling through me were too intense to contain and I yelled at the unknown man: 'You're fat! You stink! You're not my teacher and I'm not listening to you!'

The punishment for my tantrum was swift and I was sent straight to the principal's office. No one considered that my outburst was the result of so much fear I carried inside myself at all times. I had already started being a product of what my home life was creating without even knowing it.

The terror I held in my little heart was taking control of my reactions. I didn't stop to think about the consequences, I was in survival mode.

I was scheduled to visit the school dentist van. I arrived at school with a signed permission slip from my parents, but to say I was excited about it would be an understatement. It was just before lunchtime when an older student arrived at my classroom holding a note with my name on it – it was my turn.

I followed the older girl to the van in the middle of the school. It was close to the oval, covered by grass that was all dry and burnt from the sun and lack of rain. I remember the red dirt blowing around in the winter winds. The moment I opened the flimsy door to the van and stepped inside, a sense of danger gripped my body. I was surprised by this involuntary wave of terror that came out of nowhere and my eyes darted around the small waiting area to see if there was something I needed to run away from. All I could see was another girl, just a little bit older than me, with very pale skin and beautiful long red hair braided in a plait to one side. As I sat across from her, I felt a chill run through me as the sterile smell of disinfectant assaulted my nostrils.

A chubby dental assistant with curly blonde hair that bounced above her shoulders opened the internal door and smiled pleasantly.

'Next please.'

I looked at the girl across from me and saw she had remained glued to her seat.

'You were here before me. It's your turn,' I prompted her. *That's the usual order of things, isn't it?*

She did not budge.

'It's okay, you go first,' she said in a soft voice, barely raised above a whisper. The dental assistant threw the rules out of the window, raising her eyebrows at me in a manner that suggested I follow her into the next room. Ever the people pleaser, I did as I was told.

The dentist was a tall, slim man with very dark hair.

'Hello Janelle,' he said after looking up from his paperwork and staring directly into my eyes.

'Please have a seat in this chair for me.'

His expression was unsettling; his mouth was smiling at me, but the joy didn't reach his eyes. It was as if he was looking straight through me. I followed his instructions and the chubby assistant placed one of those disposable paper bibs on my chest, affixing it with a metal clip she slid behind my neck. She then announced she had to leave to get more supplies. She held my hand and looked me directly in the eyes: 'Don't worry little one, I'll be back soon.'

There was a sound of urgency in her voice that my nine-year-old mind didn't comprehend at the time. But in the myriad moments when I've replayed this situation through my healing journey as an adult, it was clear that she knew what she was potentially leaving me with. He wasn't a school dentist – he was a monster.

The door closed and I remember looking at my jumper. It was white and had a cat laying on a bench that was positioned across my chest. There were three mice below the cat attached to puppet strings and it was clear the cat was controlling them. The dentist looked surprised when he saw the design and made a joke about how the 'pussy liked to play'.

He placed his hand on a mouse as he spoke, then touched each of the mice and traced the line of the strings up to the cat. Frozen in my own skin, I didn't know what to do or what to say. I knew this wasn't normal behaviour, but I was just a child and didn't comprehend the seriousness of the situation. He must have seen the panic start to grow in my eyes, because he cautioned that if I made any noise, I'd be in lots of trouble.

'You don't want that, Janelle,' he said.

I breathed a sigh of relief as he stopped moving his hands up my jumper and finally checked my teeth. When he was finished, I thought I could get up and leave... but he had different ideas. Before I could sit up, he slipped his hand under my jumper and he began touching me. He groped at my childlike chest and moved down to my groin. Parts that should never be touched by anyone.

The back door swung open unexpectedly. *The assistant is back!* Relief flooded my body as the dentist automatically recoiled and he barked at me to get back to class. I didn't hesitate and ran out of there past the girl with long red hair, with tears pouring from my eyes. With the dentist's threat still ringing in my ears, I tried my best to pull myself together before I got back to class. But I was terrified. I knew I couldn't tell my parents even if I wanted to – they'd probably say I was making up stories and I'd get punished. I couldn't handle being hit for telling the truth.

Fortunately, the big lunch bell had just rung, so everyone went out to play. I sat quietly in the undercover area and tried my best to disappear. My attempts were futile, however. A teacher approached me with a note telling me to go to the principal's office. The teacher took me there and as I walked with her across the basketball courts, I was taunted by the older boys saying, 'Ooooo little white gin's in trouble! Ha-ha you're going to get it.'

When I reached the office, I found the girl with long red hair sitting in there, along with my mum and the deputy principal.

'Take a seat Janelle,' the deputy principal instructed. She wasn't harsh, but I could tell from the tone of her voice that somehow, they all knew what had happened. *I didn't tell!* My mind raced, already terrified of the consequences for breaking the dentist's instructions. My mum had a horrified look on her face, and I started to cry.

'I did nothing wrong mum! Please don't be mad and don't tell dad!'

Mum and the deputy principal began talking. I watched as their mouths moved, but what they were saying, I couldn't tell you. I was paralysed by thoughts of what had happened and what would happen next. My next memory was being taken to the police station. I was asked many questions and I answered all of them, but at the same time, was so frightened I could barely breathe. My mother didn't even hold my hand. She sat there with her arms and legs crossed and occasionally glanced at me with this look of sadness and disbelief.

When we walked out, she put her arm around me for the first time that afternoon – although it wasn't in a comforting manner; more to hurry me towards the car.

'Janelle, I'm taking you to your Nanna's house for a while. She'll know how to help you and will know how to look after you. I just don't know what to do with you.'

I sat in the front seat of the car looking out the window with tears rolling down my face. I didn't say a word, even trying to quieten my sniffles. All I wanted was for my mum to wrap me up in her arms and never let me go, but she was sending me away instead.

We arrived at my Nanna's house and she was waiting for me at the top of the stairs, arms reached out to me. My desire for my mother's affection seemed to melt away and I managed a smile. I was finally safe and in a place I was loved. Nanna took me into the spare room, which we called the grandchildren's room. There were so many beds in there and it was filled with memories of laughter I'd shared with Nanna and my cousins. The smell of potpourri and moth balls was comforting and wrapped me in a protective cloak. But there was a very different energy around us that day.

Nanna sat with me on one of the old steel framed single beds with a knitted blanket and talked me through everything. She told me it wasn't anything I did and I had nothing to be ashamed about. She handed me a tiny teddy she had made and said, 'Janelle, this is your trauma teddy. Hold it and love it, tell the teddy all about your sadness and pain.' Then she held me and allowed me to be a child.

I love her more than anything in this world and I am forever grateful for how she took me in and made me feel truly safe for the first time in three years.

Chapter 3

Darkness Descends

As much as I wanted to stay with Nanna, my time with her was always going to be temporary. I dreaded the day when I had to return home, back to the shadows that were no doubt still lingering.

It wasn't long before my father had another trigger and the beatings began again. The man I called 'Dad' – it is a term I use very loosely these days – but he rationalised his actions by telling me, 'You are the strongest one and the eldest, so you can take it!'

Interestingly, I don't actually recall a single moment where I hated him during my childhood. I was terrified and haunted by him and I never felt safe, but it was many years before that would fester into hatred. I so desperately wanted to please both my parents so that they would, in my eyes, just be happy and love me.

While he never touched a hair on my sister's heads, it wasn't just me that he would fight with. He had two older brothers, an older sister, and a younger sister. I can clearly recall one night there was a family barbecue at our house and it ended in a horrific fight between the brothers. All the women tried to rush all the children into the house, but I saw everything from the window. In a way, I was intrigued by it all. To see it from an outsider's perspective instead of being the one on the receiving end.

It was a very violent fight. One brother had the top of his ear bitten off and another was getting pulled over a tin fence, slicing right around his armpit. The yelling and punching was terrifying. My dad was put in a straitjacket that night and taken away. I don't have any memory of anyone talking about it. It was as if there was an unspoken rule that no one would dare talk about it, almost like it was accepted.

There was only one night I can remember where my dad laid a hand on my mother in an aggressive way. I was around ten years old and he was drinking. He was drunk enough that mum was very annoyed with him and poured out his beers. He came up the back stairs and in through the back door, stumbling around and accusing mum of tipping his beers out. My mother could see the rage beginning to build and denied it, but this only served to make him angrier. My sisters and I were sitting at the dining table with a clear view to the kitchen and we saw my father pick her up by her throat and shove her into the cupboards above her.

My sisters were terrified, but I didn't even hesitate. The moment he lifted her up, I ran over and started trying to pull him off of her. He looked at me strangely, and thinking back it was like a mix of surprise and almost pride that he recognised this inner strength within me. But this passed in a flash as he kicked me away. I ran for the phone and called my Poppy, knowing he would be able to provide us with some sense of safety that night. I paid for my act of bravery once Poppy had left.

I became adept at reading people's emotions. It was necessary for me to be able to survive. I was always nervous around my dad, especially if he was in a mood. I could sense my mother's fear before I heard his heavy footsteps in the hallway. My breath would quicken and my stomach would churn as those footfalls landed closer to my bedroom door. I would assess my situation and see if it was best to try to escape to my favourite tree in the backyard or simply find a hiding spot in my room. Then, I would wait.

If he walked past, I knew I'd be okay. If there was a noise that woke him, or something or someone upset him, I'd panic. He'd see my innocent little body as a target to release an anger that he could not control any other way. So I'd again retreat into myself, blocking out the pain and tasting the salty tears that flowed from my eyes in reaction to the paralysing horror that would take over. *Just make it stop please! PLEASE take me away to a place where I won't be scared anymore.*

I'd lay on the bottom of the bathtub with cold water washing away the ugliness from beating after beating. It became the 'normal' way of life and I was slowly becoming desensitised to it and to life itself. As with any cycle of abuse, there were periods of relative harmony, where my father would buy me lovely things and put money under the door, which I may have locked and barricaded with whatever I could find. But the routine got old and I no longer felt special to the first man I loved.

At the time, it felt like I was dancing in the hot red dirt with the darkness, but I was actually growing stronger every day and in every way.

When I was eleven, we moved to Emmalyn Close, Soldiers Hill. It was just over three kilometres away from our previous home, across the Leichhardt River, but far enough away that my sisters and I had to change schools. My experience with my grade 4 teacher was clear proof that I fought any change that I didn't choose for myself. My heart raced at the mere thought of having to navigate a new environment and find new safe spots. I had no choice but to go.

With both of my parents working in the mines, the new house felt so big. It had pale mint green internal brick walls, colourful curtains and white tiled floors. It felt like a palace compared to the house we came from. Despite my previous anxiety, this excited my sisters and I because there was so much room to play and feel free.

My room was the first room, diagonally across was my youngest sister's room then down the back was my middle sister's room, closest to mum and dad's. The main bathroom was tiled all black with a silver marbled streak. Little did I know then, but I would come to know that bathroom like the back of my hand – it would become my lockdown room.

A few weeks after moving in, my father had a surgical procedure on his back. The recovery was prolonged and painful and for six weeks I heard him crying and yelling in pain as he lay down in bed. The thoughts I had were dark. *Now could be my time to get him back! We could be rid of him forever!* There was a never-ending war in my mind that swung between my desire for revenge and empathy for him and his pain. Ultimately, it was fear that prevented me from acting on any of it. Despite being bedridden, he continued to yell at us a lot and I wondered what would happen if he did get up. It was Mum who bore the brunt of his verbal abuse at this time and I wondered why she continued to let him talk to her like that. I just wanted her to be happy and strong, but she always chose to keep the peace and enabled his darkness.

Not long after my father recovered, he went out with his brother to a local sporting bar and returned home very intoxicated. That night, the level of fear, hatred, pain, and anger I felt was elevated to a whole new level. I was sleeping in my bed and all of a sudden, the stereo in my room started playing AC/DC so loud it woke the whole house. My tired, scared eyes peering up at him weren't enough to stop him. I asked him to turn it down and the words had barely left my mouth before I was pulled out of bed by my torso and thrown up against the brick wall. I was smashed against that wall again and again. My mother was standing at my doorway, holding my two younger sisters back while crying for him to stop. She was paralysed in pain watching and couldn't help me; she didn't know how to. *How can she stand by and watch?* I looked at her and my sisters, feeling so lost. I was just a little girl myself. I needed help and protection. Her weakness enabled him to continue to take out on me the pain and ugliness he felt for himself. It was like no one heard my screams, no one saw my pain, and no one was there to save me, to hold me, and to love me.

Imagine screaming but feeling like you had no sound, no voice. All I could do was look at my mother and sisters and wish it would stop.

When his rage was satisfied, he dropped me to the floor and left without another word. My sisters came running to me, covering me with their bodies, crying with me. They took me to the bathroom and told me to hide in there and lock the door. 'We love you!' they whispered as they shut the door.

They knew my father could easily snap once more that night and they wanted to keep me safe. So, I did just that. I stayed there for hours that night on the bottom of a cold bathtub.

After beatings like this one, I would black out for a bit simply from trauma. I have no recollection of how long the blackouts would last for. On this occasion, I came back into awareness to the sweet sounds of my sisters' voices calling to me from outside the bathroom door in the morning. As I opened the door, they took both my hands and we went to my room and sat together on my bed. They handed me a photo of the three of us and on the back, they wrote me a message each.

The first message read, 'I don't want to see you hurt anymore, please remember me.' The second read, 'You'll always be my sister, please remember me. We love you, big sis.' It was like they had this inner knowing that on some level they were losing me as my spirit was being broken. I still have the photo to this day.

All I could think was if two young girls can feel the danger and sadness, where was my mother's love and protection? Instead, she would cover my bruises up and tell me if I said anything to anyone, I'd get taken away from the family, and then I'd have nothing. At times that didn't feel like it would be such a bad thing. I used to think *All I want is to be anywhere else,* so her words didn't scare me. What it ultimately meant was that I could not trust my mother. How could I? To me, she allowed the violence to continue. I never knew if she was even trying to make it safer for me. It was like she had given up on me as soon as the beatings began when I was six years old.

Year 7 at my new school was my favourite. I made lifelong connections with people that I still have in my life to this day. There were nine girls in our group and the friendships we made were magical, full of love and support. We all had regular sleepovers, although I never had them at my place because I was terrified of what might happen if dad was angry and my friends were there to see him beat me – or worse, be beaten as well.

Monique and I were super close. We did everything together. I loved being at her house because her home was filled with the warmth of a real family, who loved each other and were genuinely connected to one another. They would eat dinner together, laugh together, talk about their problems and just had so much respect for each other. It was everything I dreamed my own home life could be. Monique's friendship saved me in so many ways. I learnt to trust and felt like a child, free to explore and create memories. We'd ride our bikes to school along a bike path, stopping at the corner store for bags of lollies and giggling over the silly stories we'd tell each other.

We'd confide in each other about the boys we had crushes on and planned things to do on the weekends. Once we both got home from school, we'd make a phone call to each other. She was my safety person.

We also had a very beautiful friend Haily, whom we'd nicknamed 'shorty'. Haily was the smallest in our group, but she had such a big heart and her laughter was infectious. If there were ever any arguments between the girls, she'd just say it was natural and not get involved. Haily had a knowingness about her that I felt drawn to.

We all went on Grade 7 camp together at Lake Tinaroo, just past Cairns, where we were told of a ghost that haunted the camp grounds. There was an old locked up area full of bunk beds, all covered in a thin layer of dust and an old red dusty child's tricycle sitting out front. We'd have each other so scared of the stories we'd make up that we'd huddle close together. We'd run through the grounds laughing with our classmates and explore. I felt lighter than I'd ever felt. I was carefree and felt safe. There were kids that were homesick, but for me I'd never been happier than in that moment.

Haily's aunty came and picked her up from camp, as she was going to catch up with some of her family for a few days, then she'd return to camp and come back on the bus with us to Mt. Isa. When she left we all felt sad; it just wasn't the same without her.

Little did we know, this was one of the last times we'd all be together. The year finished when we all graduated primary school. We had a school dance and celebrated together. There were two high schools nearby and we weren't all going to the same one.

I had my thirteenth birthday party the January after school finished. It was one of the birthdays all my family and friends were at. It was such a fun party. We had a big pool, a table tennis table and a massive back yard to run in and enjoy the celebrations. We all had our first boyfriends and we were enjoying the feeling of growing up.

My dad was drinking lots that night, but he behaved himself. There were times he'd get loud and I'd feel stressed about whether he would go to his dark place, but it was loudness from a happy place. For once, I laughed with him. I saw the love he had for me and how he just wanted to see me happy.

The new school year started and it was scary, but I had my bestie Monique with me, so everything was going to be okay. A few months later, Haily passed away from brain cancer. The feeling of losing my best friend at such a young age shattered my heart and soul. I went to her viewing and saw her peaceful little body just looking like she was sleeping. We all put a gift in with her as we said our goodbyes. We were so brave; we held each other so tightly. We cemented bonds together that day that would last for the rest of our lives.

Chapter 4

Misdirected Anger

I began to lie to my parents and say I had more than one basketball training session and I played more than one game on Friday afternoons – just so I could avoid home. My mother never questioned me. I knew she knew I was lying but I guess in a way, it was her way of keeping me safe. It was one of the only ways she ever did, so I was grateful she played along.

I started training with the older teams and soon was selected for regionals and rep teams. My dedication to sport as a way out of the darkness that waited for me at home started to pay off. The happy benefit was that this meant more training and even trips away from home to compete.

It was very expensive – to travel from the outback to anywhere was a big trip – but money at this stage wasn't a problem. Both my parents worked in the mines and we had an abundance of wealth, so my mum just paid for it all.

My coach Naomi soon caught on to what was happening at home. To me, she was the first person outside of our four walls who actually knew what was happening. Of course, now that I am an adult, I've learned there were family members who knew, but were warned not to intervene. My grandfathers and one of my grandmothers tried their best to protect me from a distance, always just keeping an eye on me. Naomi would push me harder on the days I was exhausted from being up all night, as she knew it was healthier for me to get it out on the court than to bottle it all up.

From having her unconditional silent support, I got tough! I mean, really tough. Some might say stupidly brave.

I was a young teenager at this stage and I had so much hate and anger built up in me, I didn't know what to do with it. I didn't know who I was and I didn't care about myself or the people around me. I started yelling back at home, ducking the hits and even hitting back. None of it made me feel good, but it was a release.

I turned aggression into deep passion for my sport and played up a grade against the big tough girls. I took on every one of them with fearless abandon. Sure, there were plenty of times I came off second best, but physical pain felt numb to me, so I knew I could get back up and keep going.

One day, my mum came to watch a game. I felt like she had started to begrudge the closeness I had with Naomi and wanted to confront her. Little did my coach know, the evening before was a really dark one. I didn't tell anyone, even though both eyes were bruised and grab marks were still visible on my arms.

When Naomi saw me, she held me so tight and declared I would be staying at her house.

'Enough is enough!' she said. She asked me if I still wanted to play and I didn't hesitate to say yes and told her my mother was here to see her as well. I knew I could trust her, so I didn't mind them talking. Naomi approached my mum, asking if they could chat after the game.

It was a hot afternoon. The basketball courts were made of bitumen and the sun would heat them up like crazy, so much so, the soles of your shoes would stick – that's how hot it was that day.

The game started. I ran to the other end of the basketball court and my nose popped! Blood flowed and the game had to be stopped. I was taken to the first aid office and that's where it started. My coach was the first to me, then mum came in yelling and crying, putting all the attention on herself with her crocodile tears. Naomi took mum outside. Words flowed as emotions ran on an all-time high.

My mum didn't want the truth to come out; she was scared about what might happen.

This was the woman who couldn't stand up to the man that slowly but surely took my innocence from me, yet she was happy to have a go at my coach. It was clearly a jealousy issue for her. Her insecurities and guilt were consuming her and led her to overcompensating in front of others. Let's just say, mum got her just desserts and I felt so thankful to Naomi for being my advocate.

That sense of peace passed in the blink of an eye, because not one word was said on the car trip home. It wasn't until we pulled into the driveway that mum said, 'Shower Janelle, then go to your room. I'll call you for dinner.'

That day was never spoken about again, I went on training and going away for rep trips, but anger just kept growing inside me. I started behaving badly and didn't care about the consequences.

For one basketball representative trip we went to a small town called Burdekin, just outside of Townsville. We were billeted out in pairs to families. Kelly and I were together. I was so happy about this as she was one of my best friends. One night, the eldest girl of the family we were staying with started taunting Kelly calling her names like 'fatty, big legs, bad breath Kelly'. Those words really hurt my friend.

'Don't worry, I'll make sure she gets it on the court tomorrow,' I promised.

As fortune would have it, we were set to play her team.

Prior to the bullying, the girl had confided in us that she had a crush on Aaron, one of my mates. I took it upon myself to embarrass her by telling everyone how she felt towards Aaron, knowing full well that this would annoy her greatly. I didn't care, what could she do to me? She took her jogger off her foot and threw it at my head.

This was the first time I remember that feeling of 'snapping.' Something came over me that I had never experienced. I launched at her with tightly clenched fists and started hitting her. She was throwing some good hits back. I had my rep team shirt on at the time, so when we were taken to head of department, I was told I couldn't play another game during that tournament.

I felt shame and guilt for letting my team down, but that's where the poor-me emotions stopped. The satisfaction of knowing I stood up for someone I cared about, no matter what the circumstances, felt amazing. I was not going to be like my mother; I would protect the people in my life that I cared about. I never initiated violence, but I also wasn't scared to use force to stand up for what I believed in. I had then, and still have today, a strong sense of righteousness.

Chapter 5

A Painful Loss

I started to gain confidence, which is something a child of abuse rarely has. But I had an inner strength growing and I fuelled that feeling with anger. I'd hardly be at home, always playing with the kids in the street or playing basketball. I only had to stick up for myself a few times at school, as the friends I had made were the kinds of kids no one messed with. I had transformed from a scared little girl into a street-smart young woman.

I had a good time for about six months. Then I spoke back to my dad in front of some of his mates. Big mistake. You see, it wasn't just the physical abuse that would terrify me, it was the tone either of my parents used when they incessantly yelled and screamed, sometimes for hours on end. It would always result in doors slamming or holes being punched in walls. The level of abuse that took place in my house of shadows was at epic proportions. The moment a voice was raised, I instantly went into my shell again, with no sign of the strong girl who emerged when my feet hit the pavement outside our house. I had bottled up everything; it was like I swallowed all the pain and it slowly ate me from the inside out.

With my anxiety at a new all-time high, I developed an eating disorder. At least, this is what the doctors labelled me with. I didn't believe them. It was again just a way my mother would try and convince me there was something wrong with me. My body was filled with sadness, fear, anger, low self-respect and anxiety. I felt eating 'their' food was just going to keep poisoning me. To me, it was my body's way of rejecting their toxins. Every time I ate, I would vomit until my stomach was empty.

My mum thought I was busy sticking my fingers down my throat. The truth was, I simply couldn't stomach anything anymore. My parents made me sick. My life made me sick. As I had experienced since I was a child, I wondered *who is out there who will listen to me? Who can help me? How can I turn my life around?*

I connected with an amazing girl on my basketball team. Her name was Stevi. She was escaping her life at home, too. Our friendship grew very close very quickly and Stevi has been by my side ever since.

My dad was made redundant from the mines, and we sold everything and moved to Hervey Bay. The day we flew out was such a sad day for me. Moving to the beach lifestyle from the bush and mixing with different kids was such a big change. *How am I going to cope?*

I fought the change with all my might and within six months, the only man who ever stepped in front of my dad's fists – my Poppy – died. In his final hours, he had the hospital staff call my parents' house, requesting that my dad and I go see him. I was woken with this news in the early hours of the morning. If my Pop wanted me, I'd be there – nothing would stop me.

I played the organ from when I was very young. Music was a way of escaping the ugliness at home and allowed me to create something beautiful with my emotions.

Pop was my biggest fan. When he first went into hospital, I made a cassette for him with all his favourite songs on it. He looked so frail as I stepped into that hospital room the morning we were summoned.

'My girl, come here and sit with me,' he said, patting the spot beside him on the bed. He always called me that. The entire family called me his change-of-life baby. My Pop never touched a drop of alcohol once I was born.

'This child will never see me living the life I've lived,' he told the family.

He was my whole world and I was his. Pop's wife, Gran, was jealous of his love for me. She always resented me and would call me 'little bitch'. But I still loved my Gran; I didn't understand the depth of jealousy she had towards me until I was older.

Pop reached out his aged, weathered arm and squeezed my hand with all of his strength. A tear rolled down his cheek as he said, 'My girl, your Pop has to go, but you must know that bastard won't hurt you ever again.'

As he said those words, he looked at my dad and said, 'Did you hear me boy? Never hurt her again.' Without missing a beat, he followed up with, 'Boy, I need to piss. Get the container.' Dad obeyed and Poppy moved his hips with a big jolt, exploding into a fit of laughter.

'Ha-ha! I pissed on you! I told you I would before I died.'

It did well to lighten the mood and speaks to his true larrikin nature. But I seriously hoped that dad got the message. *Time will tell, I guess.*

A few hours later, Poppy passed away. This was the start of some of my darkest days, weeks, months and years.

I was fifteen now and thought I knew everything about everything. Little did I know then, I had a lot to learn. My Poppy's funeral was the worst day of my life. The heavy red curtains were pulled around Poppy's coffin and then I heard this faint voice of a sweet little girl saying, 'Poppy I love you. I made this for you, so you think of me. Enjoy, my Poppy. Love, your girl.'

It hit me so hard, like a shock wave of gut-wrenching sadness when I realised that little girl was me. I felt utterly disconnected from what was happening around me. I fell out of my chair and was unable to stand as the pain gripped my body and I forgot how to breathe. The panic, fear and sadness were too much to handle.

I don't even remember leaving the funeral parlour, but the next thing we were all back at my parent's house for the wake. I couldn't deal with all the fake happy stories. My Pop really had strong views on life and while he had no problems with religion, he always said he never wanted those 'bloody nuns at his wake talking shit about God'. I loved him for who he was and as he was once the protector of me, I now felt I had to protect him.

I went out to the front of my parents' house and as I ran through the concrete arches at the front entrance, I stopped still. An overwhelming sense of hate and anger flooded me and I started punching the brick wall. The world around me went silent and I couldn't stop. An older cousin of mine pulled me away from the wall. When I looked at my hands, knuckles cut open and the rich dark red blood running down my forearms, I realised that I felt nothing. I was completely numb to the reality of what had just happened and was lost in a world of internal and external pain.

The next few months were just a big blur of wandering around the dark places in my mind and trying not to drown in the darkness. All I wanted was to be held and loved, to heal through this nightmare. My mum would constantly say she felt she couldn't keep me safe anymore and ask what was wrong with me.

Instead of listening to his father's dying wish, the violence between my dad and I was getting worse. I had quit school and was enrolled at TAFE in the hairdressing unit. My Nanna was visiting and I overheard a conversation with my mother, who was crying and saying she didn't know what else to do with me and how she never really knew what to do with me. I felt so lost and hearing my mother say those words, they broke the last remaining fragment of our relationship.

Nanna came to me and said, 'Janelle dear, your mum and I need to take you for a drive. Your mum needs my help to help you, love.'

'Where are we going, Nan?' There was no response, just bustling activity to get me into the car. Next thing we arrived at the Centrelink office and were greeted by a welfare and youth worker. All types of paperwork were passed in front of me between my mum and the case workers and I remained in the dark about everything that was unfolding. My stomach was in knots with the uncertainty of it all.

Finally, they started to talk to me about being signed over to the government system until I was sixteen, then I would be classed in a different category that meant I could work and get Austudy and rent assistance.

When I asked them to explain what was really happening, mum started to cry and she kept saying, 'Janelle I'm sorry, I don't know what else to do.'

Nanna explained I was still my parents' daughter but to keep me safe from the dangers at home and to try and save my parents' marriage, mum and dad had decided to no longer be my legal guardians.

The room started to shrink and the walls felt like they were closing in on me. The pressure of my pounding heartbeat was becoming so overwhelming that I thought I was going to burst. But then, it all faded away. Like somehow I had turned off all my emotions and completely disconnected to the world and everyone around me.

What am I meant to do? Where am I going to live? How am I going to pay for everything?

My mum gave me all my clothes and an old single bed. No cupboards, no money, no car... nothing. I moved into a place my friends shared. They were older than me and into some pretty hard party days. My room was their laundry – an oversized, rudimentary outdoor area that was barely enclosed. There was absolutely no privacy, with my room essentially a shared space. My clothes were kept in cardboard boxes I stuck on top of each other and covered with a sheet.

I was earning $110 a week in a hairdressing apprenticeship with an extra top up payment every second week from Austudy. I lived on two-minute noodles and toasted cheese sandwiches for twelve months, before I had to leave the toxic environment. There was a massive party one night and a car was stolen. Most of the people at the house were affected by a concoction of drugs and alcohol and it made me so angry that I was stuck there.

I wanted change, but I had no mentor or guidance. I was young and scared and had no one to turn to. So, one day I packed my stuff and called my mum. It was one of the hardest things I've done as the fear of rejection when I heard her voice was so intense.

The first thing she said was, 'Well that didn't last long! Where are you going to live now?' I asked If she would let me stay at the family home until I found somewhere. I was told I could stay, but at the first signs of dad getting angry, I'd be shown the door.

'Why am I to blame? Why am I punished for dad's behaviour?' I demanded.

'You two can't live together and your sisters and I don't need it!'

Once again, I wondered how she could stand up and act protectively of my sisters and my dad, but yet in all these years, she never protected me.

'Whatever.' I resigned myself to her conditions. *I just need a place to stay for a while. Hopefully we can all get along for long enough.*

I missed my sisters. But it wasn't long before I realised they had grown closer to one another since I'd left home. I didn't recall where I fit into their lives. They used to look at me like they wanted to protect me, but now their faces looked at me like I was a warrior. They used to tell me stories of what it was like when I wasn't at home and share things the family had said about me. When I'd do my makeup, they would sit in the bathtub just watching me and learning how to use makeup themselves.

There was something they did learn from seeing what I went through – they learned ways to gain what they needed or wanted in life by being sneaky. If they ever got caught, they would somehow turn the limelight back on me so that it would diffuse their situation. They had actually crafted ways to put me in the way of the anger. Perhaps they, on a subconscious level, thought I would shield them and keep them safe.

My dad called me out of the blue one evening all flustered.

'Girl! I need your help. Your little sister is at a party and I'm about to lose it.'

I was so protective of my sisters and I knew what dad was capable of, so I said I'd go with him to Maryborough, which was twenty-five minutes away. At the young age of fourteen, my sister had become sexually active. I remember the shame on my dad's face and the disgust as he told me that.

My sister didn't seem to be the slightest bit concerned her secret was out there. This same sister hit the party drugs at a young age and was pregnant at seventeen, having her first child at eighteen years. I never did anything like that. My mother protected and overcompensated for my two sisters' behaviour and enabled them to act like this. All I kept thinking was, *Far out if that were me, I'd be beaten to a pulp.*

The following Christmas, my middle sister had moved out with a group of friends to a share house and, like me early on, trying to people please was her coping strategy in life. She let herself into the family home and stole all the food that mum had bought for Christmas and all the bedding off of my bed. To this day, I have no idea why she took my bedding. I saw my mother cry and she kept asking, 'Why would Alice do this?' She knew how hard mum worked to provide the food she did that year. Without dad's income, the carefree financial days had passed for my parents. My dad was cranky and even said to me, 'Gubby you've never even done anything like this and girl, I know I've given it to you.'

That single comment felt so validating. I just nodded my head.

Chapter 6

An Escape

I met a guy called Ian at the basketball club. He was strong and kind, someone I felt I was safe with. I loved that. I watched his games and he'd watch mine. We would go to the same parties and he made me laugh. I felt free when I was with him, like I could truly be myself.

I started living with a girlfriend's parents for a while, so I could have a roof over my head. But as I began spending more and more time with Ian, I moved in with him and his mum Sue.

I had never known the love of a mother like Sue and from the very beginning, she took the time to listen and showed compassion for my journey in life to that point. I would spend many nights laying on the couch in front of them, just talking to Sue and taking her advice on board as I started the road of healing.

I was soon to turn eighteen. I had an apprenticeship in

hairdressing and I loved every second of my job. Ian allowed me to be me, even though at times I was so down I couldn't bear to face the world. The hate in my heart was eating me slowly from deep within. Other days I would be so full of life I could pinch myself. But it wasn't long before the anger would wash over me and this cycle would repeat itself.

My health started to decline to the point where I was fainting randomly and wouldn't have any recollection of the events leading up to it. At the time, I was oblivious to the underlying cause. I realise now it was depression and it had hold of me so tightly with its dark powers, my only way of escaping was blanking out.

I was in the salon one day and remember feeling lost, dazed and confused and then the next thing I knew, I was in the back of an ambulance. My dad was across the road when he saw me getting put into the ambulance and I saw him run to me. The look of worry on his face, seeing me so vulnerable – not as a result of his own actions for once – frightened the life out of him. He followed me to hospital. All my vitals were fine, yet I wasn't very responsive. The doctors ran tests and everything kept coming back fine, apart from low blood pressure, which wouldn't ordinarily have such an extreme effect.

When my dad heard everything was above board, he got up and left. I don't remember how long it was till I saw him again, but it was a while. I thought I was going mad, loopy, even nuts as I knew how I felt, but there was no reason medically as to why I was struggling.

Knowing what I know now, I had serious depression and it was killing me. My mental health was challenged many times and somehow, I kept picking myself up. There were a handful of times I just wanted to end my life and start a new one. Ian knew all of this and wasn't surprised when I said I had to get out of town for a while. At this stage, he was living in Sarina and working for a family friend who was like an uncle to him. He asked his boss, if I could get a job on-site doing all the cleaning, shopping and deliveries of parts and so on.

When he agreed to take me on, I thought *Excellent! This is the fresh start I need.*

I booked a bus ticket and was excited about the future. My mum wanted to drop me to the bus stop and I had no other way to get there, so I agreed. When I got out of the car and grabbed my single bag – this was all I had in the world – she handed me a card and said, 'Don't open it Janelle, till you're on the bus.'

Ever the obedient child, I found my seat on the bus and waited until the door closed and the wheels began to turn before I opened it. I looked at my mum's face as the bus slowly drove away. There was a real sense of loss in her eyes, even though I believe mum knew she'd lost me long before this. I believe seeing me on the bus, leaving the life I'd known, made her realise there wasn't anything more she could do to get me back.

I opened the card and was shocked by the words she'd written. I had never heard her utter anything like this to me directly, so it felt foreign to think they came from her hand.

> *Janelle,*
>
> *Now you are safe and now you are free, just always remember me and know I tried.*
>
> *I do love you.*
>
> *Mum.*

Tears slowly rolled down my face as I finished reading the brief note, but as I looked out the window again, she had left. In true Janelle style, I took a deep breath and looked forward, despite not knowing where I was going and how I was going to cope with whatever came next.

I arrived in Mackay late that afternoon and Ian was there with the biggest smile and open arms. I felt safe again. It was such a beautiful feeling. At first, we had a house in Sarina, which was the first real house I could make my own.

Ian worked long hours and none of the other men's partners lived in the area, so I tried to get a part-time hairdressing apprenticeship, but was unsuccessful. I decided to let it go for a bit and work hard for Ian to make some decent money.

I met some beautiful people, with whom I had such an amazing time going on adventures like motorbike riding, quad bike beach riding, camping, rock jumping and parties. Karaoke was a regular event at an old pub at the bottom of a winding range where everyone wore flannelette shirts, jeans and cowboy hats. All drinking ice-cold beers and telling stories of their days and their lives. They all had a story and I was having the best time listening to them. I felt I did not have a care in the world.

Then Ian came home and said at the end of our lease we would be moving to the camp site they were building on-site at the top of the range. I was fine with that; I didn't mind because I got along with everyone.

Then another night, he surprised me with, 'Janelle, I think you should call your parents. It's been a long time.' Little did I know he had planned for my dad to first come visit and after he left, for my mum to come and stay. I was unsure how I felt about this at first, but it warmed my heart that Ian wanted me to rediscover a connection to family once more.

Both visits were fine; Ian went out of his way to make sure of that. For the first time, I felt maybe my parents wanted to be in my life in a positive way, so I allowed them back in. We would speak once a week after they returned home. I was scared of opening myself up to them, but at the same time, all every child wants is to be loved and protected by their parents. I was still in the process of healing from the pain they caused and to be honest, I was still surrendering my innocence to them. I just wasn't aware of it.

They were very clever at hiding their ulterior motives and whenever they came to visit me, they would talk about their fun memories of me as a child. It was as if the darkness was never there, like they were grooming me to again believe them and their lies so they could come back into my life and control it once again. To brainwash me and break me down. This started to become clear when they were one on one with me. Their stories didn't match up and it was as if they were sharing memories of two very different kids – they could have been completely made up for all I know. When they were together it was different again, as if there was an energy around them that made me feel like they were so lost within the shadows of what they had created. Their refusal to acknowledge their past treatment of me just made me even more determined not to fall for their attempts to bring me back into the family.

Life was very different living in dongas alongside the boys at the site. At first, it was all good. The long days and fun of letting our hair down afterwards was the release we all needed and seemed to create some semblance of balance. The site was so isolated and we were a crew of seven, so it was a tough gig crushing ballast for Queensland Rail.

My role was to set up the camp site and make it more liveable. We had a concrete slab put down between the large dongas.

The dongas were set up in a two by two parallel site. On one side was the boss's son Paul's main room. On the other side was the room I shared with Ian. There was a small gap, then the shower and toilet block. Adjacent to this row was the boss Henry's bedroom and office, then a gap and then the kitchen, single shower and the toilet Henry and I used.

I had to get up every morning at 4am before the camp woke and cook breakfast, make lunches and get the crew ready for the day. I then had to clean all their rooms, bathrooms and toilets, do all their shopping, all the administrative duties and run all the daily errands and be home in time to clean the inside of the cabins of the trucks and machinery. After that, I had to cook dinner, clean the kitchen and make sure there was enough ice-cold beer to go around. I set up a gym and outdoor entertainment system for the boys. I never once complained. Hard work was okay with me; it kept my mind busy.

On the occasions when there were train derailments in the middle of the night, the boys would bang on my door and hand me a shovel and headlight. I'd shovel ballast with them till the sun rose some days, then start my daily shift while they had a rest day. Ian was there with me and he was an amazing support, but my parents started to show concern for me as they thought I was getting overworked. I wasn't feeling the pressure, so I'd tell them it was okay.

Paul was in charge of the boys and he had a girlfriend back home that I know he missed greatly. Paul had a very domineering demeanour about him, and I always felt a little uncomfortable when I was around him. Things suddenly took a strange turn, from working hard, playing hard, and being accepted as one of the crew. Paul started to pick on me and try to embarrass me and intimidate me in front of people. Ian didn't like this and he often had arguments with

Paul regarding his behaviour towards me.

One night in the middle of winter around 1.30am with a temperature of two degrees, a train derailed. This meant working through the night again, but this time after we finished Paul said to me, 'Go have a long hot shower, you deserve it. We can organise our own breakfast today.'

I wasn't going to be told twice! I was so tired and cold, I jumped at the chance. I was enjoying the feeling of the hot, steamy water running over me and felt relief that the chill that had infiltrated my bones was beginning to melt away. My eyes were closed and I had my music playing, so I didn't hear the door open.

Next thing the boss, Henry, pulled the shower screen open and started accusing me of being lazy.

'All you're good for is giving us guys something to look at!' he raged.

This verbal attack went on and on. I turned the shower off and reached for my towel. I was shocked at his accusations and when he finally paused for a second, I asked him why he felt he had the right to come into the shower and start yelling at me. 'You work for me, so I own you!'

He left the shower block just as abruptly as he had arrived. I got dressed as tears rolled down my cheeks. *Why are all men arseholes to me when I do so much for them? I never have to be asked twice, I was doing above my job description and I'm still worthless.*

I was walking back to my room when Henry came up to me and asked to speak to me in his office and to dry my tears. No one else cared.

As I made my way to his office, my mind was racing. *You fuckwit. You and your son are bullies and I don't know how your partners put up with either of you.* When you are the only female in a camp full of men you have to be tough, otherwise they'll walk all over you. I knew I had to let my rage come to the surface and stand my ground. I slammed his office door open.

'You want to see me?' I asked, bluntly. Henry didn't hold back. He started accusing me of stealing, not cooking enough, not cleaning enough and taking too long when running jobs for him. I couldn't handle taking their abusive ways and I sure as hell wasn't going to stand there and be accused of things that were absolute rubbish. When he finally finished with his ear bashing, I told him to stick his job up his arse, packed my things and left.

Ian was in the pit drilling that day, so he couldn't answer his phone. I wrote him a note and left him a voice message. When he finally got my message, he called me straight away in tears. I had unintentionally broken his heart. He would've done anything for me and he knew all the things Paul and Henry were saying were all lies.

He told me to go and stay with his mum and he'd be there on his break in a couple of days.

Sue was so understanding, but I felt a sinking feeling. I felt like an unnecessary burden for her and didn't stay long. I decided to move in with some girlfriends. Ian kept his word and came home for his break. We tried to work things out, but Henry was like a dad to Ian, Ian's dad passed away when he was a teenage boy so Paul being Ian's best friend they went through a lot together and Henry always looked out for Ian. I wouldn't stand in the way of their relationship. We ended things and just remained friends. To be honest, the emotional numbness I felt at that point had me living life as though I had blinkers on. Sometimes I was devastated we had broken up, other times our whole relationship simply felt like a distant memory that I was no longer connected to.

I was renting a room from Sam, a friend who was a single mother with a nine-year-old daughter named Scarlett. I ended up sharing a room with Scarlett, so we talked a lot, developing a strong connection. I felt for her because Sam was pretty loose, and at times she'd forget to pick Scarlett up from school. I began to pick her up from school most days and look after the house while studying my apprenticeship. She was in and out of relationships with men all the time and there was no stability at home. Scarlett was a very lost and scared little girl who was deeply confused with life. I thought to myself, *If I'm ever a parent I'll never do this to my children.*

I only lasted in that house for six months. It all became too much. It was a chain of parties and abuse in the home, as well as a little girl becoming too reliant on me. I felt it wasn't my place to be Scarlett's substitute mother when her mum was right there. I tried to address these topics with Sam, but she wouldn't hear of it. The one time I built up the courage to get serious with her, she was on a come down from big night the night before and took it way too far. She asked me to leave in not-so-pleasant terms. She was very threatening, so I had a witness with me while I moved my things out.

Fortunately, I had a girlfriend who had a room for rent, so I moved in with her. This was the most liberating time for me. I was free from all things 'men' and living with my friends Bec and Shona. It was fun living in this house; it was all girl power, which was incredibly liberating. I felt settled at home and was doing really well in my apprenticeship. I had a new car and was feeling like, at last, it was my time to breathe. I was just living day by day and building trust in people again.

Bec, Shona and I spent many nights talking till the sun came up, laughing and really getting to know one another. I was letting myself embrace the positive change. I had never gone out with either of my sisters clubbing before and so my sister Alice arranged for us to go out one night. We were at my girlfriend Sam's house getting ready for the night dancing, drinking, laughing and really enjoying ourselves. Alice took a piece of paper and a pen and wrote down my name and phone number on it. When I asked her why she did that, Alice looked at me and said, 'You've come so far Janelle, its time.' *What the fuck are you talking about?*

'Tonight is your last chance to find your Mr Right!'

Oh, I laughed until my face hurt. I thought she was positively nuts, but I went along with the fun.

We were having such a great time at the club when they called last drinks. I looked at my sister and reached for my piece of paper. There was a guy I had been dancing with on and off during the night, so I walked up to him pulled out his shirt pocket put the piece of paper in and gave him a kiss, then walked off. I didn't think much of it to be honest. I had to work the next day, which was brutal as I had a massive hangover. When I got home Bec said I had a missed call from David and he'd left his number for me.

I went all shy and gooey. I called him back and he was still in town, so we arranged to all go out for dinner. I said to Bec in a panic, 'I can't go out by myself!' and begged her to double-date with me, as I didn't really remember much from the night before. The four of us were still tired from the epic night before, so the conversation was a tad delirious. Still, we had a great time.

David and I started dating and he quickly felt like my best mate. We had an odd relationship. The chemistry was never electric on my part, but we got along great, always dining out and drinking with friends, which is what you do in your early twenties. He got along great with the girls I lived with and never minded what I did.

A few months passed and one particular evening we didn't feel like going out, but everyone else in the house did. Bec had recently asked me for a small loan so she could afford to terminate an unwanted and unexpected pregnancy. I lent it to her, but she started acting differently leading up to the night she went out. I told David there was a small part of me that didn't believe her; if it were me who was going through the emotional turmoil of a termination, I wouldn't be partying, I'd be looking after myself. Bec was always flirty with David, but he paid no attention to her ways.

This night, she came home late and was very drunk with her leg up over some guy on my car in the driveway. I didn't care that she was doing that – far out, I've done some silly things myself – I was just concerned for her after the recent events concerning her health. So, I went outside and tried to help her. She was drunk and abusive to me. I told her to pull her head in and started walking back towards the house. She started mouthing off at me. My first thought was *shut the fuck up Bec, you're making a fool of yourself,* but I didn't say anything, just kept walking.

Then she grabbed me. I wanted to punch her in the head, but instead I just pushed her away and told the girls she was with to get a handle on her. I went inside. David asked what happened and was concerned for me.

'I think it's time you moved out Janelle.'

I knew he was right. The girl power wasn't as fun as it used to be.

A few hours passed, so it was quite late in the evening. Bec had just had a shower and all seemed to be a lot calmer. I got up to go to the bathroom and was gone for all of a few minutes when I heard David yell out to me. Shona and I went into my room where we found Bec, naked on top of David saying she wanted to sleep with him.

Oh, I saw red then! I pulled her off him and accused her of lying about the abortion as she was acting like a little slut. Shona helped me get her to her own room and that was the last I heard from her that night.

The next day I went to work and came home to Bec sitting at the dining table with a group of her new friends. She stated that she wanted me out of her house that minute and to pack my things and leave. I had nowhere to go. It was late, and real estates weren't open for me to try to find something that quickly. I told her to go fuck herself and that she would pay for this. I have a real problem with people who have no backbone to talk respectfully in private, but gang up on you to make themselves feel of importance in front of others. It is such a bully mentality.

I slammed things and took no regard for her walls, windows and other household items as I packed up my things. I called David and went to his place, but I found myself homeless again. Sadly, I was getting used to this feeling of abandonment. I thought, *What have I done? I'm over this life*. But instead of falling into the arms of despair, which were waiting patiently for me, I made a choice to no longer be a victim of my past. I chose to stand up and fight back.

I became a couch surfer for a few weeks, crashing some nights at David's place and sleeping on the couches of friends on others. It did make it difficult for me to keep any sort of routine, as I was at the mercy of the household activities as to when I was afforded the peace and quiet in the living room to sleep.

'Hey, why don't you move in with me?' David piped up one evening as we were curled up together in bed. *Why not?* I thought. It was an easy decision. His parents were lovely, I had a roof over my head and food in my belly. I didn't think David and I were that serious in the relationship department, but we got along and it seemed to work. It got to the point where we wanted our own space away from his parents, so we moved into a beautiful spacious house together. I was so excited. This was the first time I had a place to call home in a long time.

David's mum would come around nearly every day to bring him food and would just hang out. I thought it was odd behaviour then but looking back it was only because I never had that sort of mother's love myself. I started talking to my parents and sisters again, but not much had changed. It was like they were stuck in a perpetual time warp. Every time I was around them, I felt like my life was literally getting sucked out of me.

I'd leave and feel dizzy, with an upset stomach and all this agitation inside me. *Why did I let them have this control? Why did I feel like this? What was wrong with me? Why didn't they love me like they loved my sisters? Was I that much of a disgrace?*

All these thoughts haunted me around the clock. I never thought I was good enough and my anxiety towards life constantly grew each and every day. There were days that I wouldn't be able to be more than a few metres from the toilet, as I had constant diarrhoea.

I went to the doctor and was tested for all sorts of things, which only played with my head more and more. Every test came back clear. *So, what the fuck is wrong with me?* I started comparing myself to everyone else, which was not my usual character. Usually, my inner rage made me not give a second thought to anyone else. I mean, why should I have cared what they thought, right?

It turned out I cared a whole lot more than I wanted to – and it was killing me.

Chapter 7

Lured Back In

I started drinking every night, getting myself into all sorts of situations. I didn't care. I had David and we were getting along fine. He knew my past and had a unique way of dealing with my rebellious nature. He had a sense of empathy about what I'd endured, but was self-absorbed by nature and genuinely didn't seem to care what I did. It was not a healthy combination.

We had a party house while everyone else in our circle was starting to grow up and settle down. We were making great money and enjoyed spending it as well – but hey, we were having fun. Christmas Day 2003 was approaching and despite my disconnection from my family, I honoured our tradition of gathering at my parents' house on Christmas Eve so we could all wake up and enjoy a Christmas morning together. Both of my sisters and their partners were there that year as well. So, to shield myself from the drama I knew would follow as the day wore on, I started playing drinking games at 5am with the boys. Why not? We left by 11am to spend the rest of Christmas with David's family and I thank God I was asleep in the early afternoon and didn't cause any collateral damage.

The following week was New Year's, and we had a massive party at David's mates place, which happened to be across the road from my parents' house. David knew what I was like and he'd just let me go. He'd do his thing and I'd do mine. One of the girls got so intoxicated and grabbed a tray of food out of the oven without a tea towel and burnt her hand badly. Me being me, I said, 'Come with me, my parents' house is across the road. They'll have some medical things for your hand in their first aid kit.' I tapped on my parents' bedroom window. Mum let us in and went back to bed.

A few minutes later, my dad came out screaming at me, slapped me across the back of my head and started abusing me about my life and threatening to sort me out one way or another. The girl with me left and I started yelling back to dad, antagonising him further. With a few drinks under my belt, I felt bolder than ever.

'Really? What are you going to do? You don't scare me, fuck off!' I ran out of the house and when I arrived back to the party, the girls kept asking me if I was okay.

I didn't understand the intensity of their questions; I grew up being treated that way. I didn't think anything much of it other than being furious and wanting another drink. They spoke to David and said to me that wasn't normal behaviour from a family. They wanted to call the police on my dad. Don't ask me why, but this made me even madder. *Who were they to want to do that for me? No one ever got involved.* I didn't know how to deal with this, so I climbed on top of the roof and started drinking in peace and quiet; anything to get away from my life of pain.

I heard all the drama below, with the boys encouraging the girls to give me a break and stay out of my business. One of my male friends came up on the roof to see me and we did flaming sambuca shots and talked until I was ready to come down. By this stage, I was very intoxicated and for some stupid reason, David's best friend thought it would be good idea to pick me up by my feet and swing me around. He'd had a few too, and misjudged the massive timber fence post, smashing my face directly into it. I broke my nose and the rest of the night was a blur.

When I woke up, I had about twenty missed calls from my parents. I didn't return them and cried to David about the embarrassment I felt over the girls wanting to call the police on my dad. He acknowledged it was a messed-up situation and expressed how he'd had growing concerns for me since we began our relationship. I was too hungover to take it all in and slept the day away. When I woke the next day, I went into the bathroom and saw the mess of my face. David said my nose was so bad that once I passed out, he and his mate tried to straighten it up for me. Apparently, I didn't even wake up, which was a good thing.

My eyes were so black, my ego was bruised and I was feeling very ashamed; I had a really busy day ahead at work, too. *Should I go in looking like this?* I debated the merits of going in versus taking a day off, but the one thing I never did was have a day off. I was always the first one there and the last one to leave. I loved hairdressing! There was something about escaping my own shitty life and focusing on someone else's that was calming to me.

So, I called my boss and told her what happened. She knew

me and my work ethic, so she said I could come in.

'How bad can it be? I'll help you cover it up with makeup,' she offered.

But the moment I showed up, she took one look at me and told me to go straight to the doctors. I didn't want to hear of it.

'Let me work with sunglasses on and I'll go after work,' I pleaded.

'No Janelle, go and get that looked at.'

I healed pretty quickly. For some reason, I always did. I turned all my energy into working and planning my twenty-first birthday party, which was in a couple of weeks. David and I put on a party at home and all our friends and David's parents were invited. But I was in two minds about whether to invite my parents after what happened on New Year's. David encouraged me to give them another chance. Looking back, I knew it was wishful thinking on my part that the millionth chance I gave them would be the one that fixed everything. I guess I am eternally the optimist. Then again, everything is beautiful in hindsight now, isn't it?

Like all twenty-first parties, drinking games were played. The party was going well and everyone was having a great time. Then it came time for speeches. Everyone's mouths dropped wide open when my dad got up to speak. I was overwhelmed with emotion. I was pleased he was going to dedicate some words to me, but also nervous about what he was going to say.

The words that came out of his mouth weren't those of a normal proud father, sharing moments filled with funny and embarrassing stories. 'Well, I never thought Janelle would still be alive today,' he said. 'So, well done. I guess if you make it to thirty, I'll have something more to say.'

With that, he sat down.

It was impossible for everyone to hide their feelings of horror and shock and I shrunk to the size of an ant as I saw it etched on every one of my guests' faces. David quickly stood up and said something to distract everyone from what just happened and tried to lift the mood back up to the same joyful energy it was at just thirty seconds beforehand.

We had a table tennis table in our family room, so all the boys went in there and started playing drinking games. To this day I don't know what started it, but the boys had their shirts off and their opponent would have to smash the ping-pong ball as hard as they could into their backs. It was clear the party was winding up, as most of the guests had left and those who remained were going a little bit bonkers. Mum tried to get Dad to leave, but he refused and said he'd get a cab home with David's mate, who lived across the road.

I took myself off to bed while David, my dad and some of the boys kept partying. I don't remember what time the night ended for them, as I had fallen into such a deep and peaceful sleep.

The next thing I remember is my sister bashing on my bedroom window trying to wake me up. My head was pounding and I felt like I was about to vomit the toxins from all that alcohol that had flowed through me just hours before. *Was I dreaming? Was she really at my window? Why didn't she call my phone? What was with all the panic?*

Convinced I was having a lucid dream, I fell back asleep. But David then nudged me, whispering, 'Someone is here.' *Oh shit, I wasn't dreaming.* I sprung out of bed and realised my sister was in fact real, and she was in hysterics. The shock of the scene before me sent me into a panic. I ran outside to her and she began screaming, 'Dad's in hospital! They didn't want me to tell you, but I had to!'

My mind conjured up a million different reasons why he would be there, but once I'd run through them all, I realised I had no idea what the hell had happened. When I quizzed my sister, she tried to fill me in through heaving sobs. It was really difficult to make much sense of it, but I understood that dad had a massive fight with one of David's friends and ended up under police watch in hospital.

She was told not to tell me, as Mum just wanted to keep me away. Mum always held me to blame anytime my dad lost his temper. Thankfully, my sister found the courage to come and tell me. I found my car keys and sped off to the hospital. I was still most likely over the legal limit to drive, but I was spurred on by my rage.

Once again, I found myself thinking: *Why was my mother blaming me and protecting him? He was the arsehole who told everyone the night before he was surprised I was still alive. FUCK HIM,* I thought. *I don't care that they don't want me in hospital, I want to see him hurting and to hear what he has to say for himself.*

I went screaming into the hospital yelling, 'Where is he? You coward old man! Hiding behind doors'. I wish I could've hidden from him during my life to avoid the abuse, but no – he always had access to me. It was frustrating that this time I couldn't get to him. They wouldn't let me in. I heard my mother instruct the staff to get me out of the hospital because it was all my fault. I stood there in silence, completely in shock at what she'd just said. *How was any of this my fault?*

I calmed myself down and the police came and spoke to me. They told me my father had been in an aggressive altercation with another male. They suggested I go home, as having me there was aggravating my father. The police were waiting for him to calm down so they could interview him; he was being questioned for starting it all. I sat there in the hospital lounge area with people staring at me and I felt like I was sinking into a big black hole, just wishing someone would magically make everything better.

Then my phone starting ringing. It was David.

'Janelle come home. I have to tell you something.'

How I was able to once again get behind the wheel, I don't know. But when I walked inside, David stood there looking shocked. He told me to call Chloe, who was with Ben, our friend who had shared the cab home with Dad and Luke. David handed me his phone and I was shaking as I called her, thinking *What am I about to hear? Only a few weeks earlier these people wanted to call the police on my dad, what will they think of me now?*

Chloe didn't waste any time and began to fill me in on what had happened.

'Janelle, your dad was sitting in the front of the cab last night and started telling the boys what he did to you as a child. About all the abuse and everything else. Luke being Luke and hating abuse to women and children, smashed your dad's head against the door frame of the cab and your dad lost it. He was swinging punches in the cab and the cab driver kicked them out at our house. At this stage they were in such an aggressive state, the cab driver called the police. Your dad was saying he was going to kill everyone and he wasn't scared. It was terrifying! We called your mum and she came over. By this time, your dad took one last massive swing at Luke. Luke dodged the punch and your dad ended up face down in the gutter. The police arrived just before Luke was about to stomp on the back of your dad's head. We were all screaming for them to stop. Ben got hurt trying to stop them both. They were just so enraged. Your dad pushed your mother and told us all to fuck off. The police took him. I'm so sorry Janelle.'

I sat there in shock. I was so mad at my father for his behaviour, and how dare my mother say it was all because of me? From what I had just heard, my father just had the shit beaten out of him because he admitted to what he did to me as a child. *How is that my fault?* My shock faded into tears. The flood of emotional release was fuelled by a life of pain, shame and abandonment. I felt so much sadness and it began to morph into anger. David called his mum to see if she could come around to help me.

I don't remember the next couple of days very well. This big secret that I had kept locked away in the house of shadows that lived within me was now known to the people around me.

I had panic attacks and my anxiety had never been higher. Growing up, I was told, 'Janelle don't you ever tell anyone anything. No one will believe you anyway. We'll say you're lying and that you like to cause trouble.'

These are the words my coward of a mother would tell me so often that I believed her. She was enabling him instead of protecting me. My mother chose to hide the truth from everyone, but why? Who was she protecting? Was it easier for her to blame me than to stand up to him? Was she that terrified herself that she sacrificed me in order to save herself?

The next few weeks were tough. David and I would visit our friends to try to get some sense of normalcy back in our lives, but I couldn't go to Luke's as it was across from my parents' house. This was the first time I really stood up for myself. Instead of being pulled back into their dangerous games, I made a choice to love myself more. It was like breaking an addiction; when you hit those lows, all you want to feel are the highs. For me, the 'drugs' were the flight or fight adrenaline and uncertainty I knew was a lifelong pattern.

It was one I was about to change in such a ground-breaking way.

Chapter 8

A Change of Scenery

With our relationship still rock solid, David and his brother had worked together to build a house. During the process, they had spoken on and off about going into business together building houses. I needed a fresh start too and our lease was almost up, so we decided to pack up everything and move to beautiful Coolum Beach.

Filled with excitement and a fresh, energised view on my life, the thought of a new future filled me with joy. David and I packed up our cars and his parents' cars and drove in convoy to the new house. I didn't even tell my parents we were moving; I still wasn't talking to them.

I found a good job and quickly moved into a management position and became head trainer at the salon. Throughout all the turmoil, hairdressing remained my creative outlet. I threw myself into my work and said yes to every opportunity. It was one of these opportunities that led me to meet a kinesiologist. Yamuna was her name and I saw her fortnightly for a period of about two years. I studied yoga with her and attended classes twice a week. I joined Fernwood, a women's only gym, and was focused on self-improvement.

The owners of the salon I worked at were a couple. The woman was nine years older than her husband and she wore the pants, so to speak. She was a very threatening lady, but I saw an opportunity to learn and grow from this. The result was that I had a different view of her than the rest of the staff. I was still battling with bouts of anxiety that affected my tummy and the severity directly related to the nervousness she created within the team. I took it all on board and I saw it as my job to protect the staff from her wicked ways. Again, I had found a way of being the sacrificial object in situations.

Peeling back the emotional layers through my work with Yamuna, I was looking within at the effects of my childhood and teenage years. I noticed a dangerous pattern. I seemed to attract love in an abusive form. You see, what you believe, becomes. I wasn't raised thinking I could achieve my dreams or be the best at anything. I spent my younger years fighting for my place and surviving.

As I started to heal, I began to think maybe my parents would be proud of me. Maybe they would love me enough to just be kind. With the aim of healing my past, I started to let them back in. David never said anything to me about this; we seemed to just peacefully coexist. He was emotionally shut off to the world and this worked for me because I didn't have to get too close to a point of heartbreak. David welcomed my parents over, but said there was to be no aggressive behaviour or they would never come back again.

I was soon sucked back into the emotional roller coaster of dealing with my parents. It wasn't long before I returned to feeling trapped and drained of all energy. Fortunately, there was 250 kilometres between us.

My health deteriorated. My endometriosis was flaring up, stress from work really started getting to me and to top it all off – I had a cancer scare. I was diagnosed with CIN 3, which is *not* cancer, but abnormal cells that have the potential to become cancer if it spreads to normal tissue nearby. I'd had abnormalities with cells before, so my doctor didn't want to take any chances and I had to have the cells burnt off and sent off for a regular screening to confirm I was in the clear.

While all of this was unfolding, David and his brother had bought another house in Buderim and his brother was living there, while David and I were in the Coolum house. Their building work started to dry up and the financial pressures were mounting. They decided to sell both houses and go their separate ways. It made sense; with the burden of mortgages gone, they could focus on their business.

David bought a boat with his money and paid off our debts. I was referred to a gynecologist for further tests. I asked David to come along, as we always ended up arguing after a medical appointment because he didn't understand what I was saying when I tried to recall the information given to me by the specialists. We sat there with the specialist and he read through my results. My heart pounded as I feared the worst.

Dr Weaver said my fertility was compromised and even though I was only twenty-three years old, he highly recommended if I wanted children to have them now. I'd need treatment to conceive as it was, and this would only get worse as I got older. *Children? Wait! What? Now? Me? David? Wow!* He asked David and I how long we had been together and at that stage it was about four years. David was twenty-nine at the time and I remember looking at him, trying to figure out what he was thinking. I wished I could somehow crawl into his mind and just get a straight answer.

It was a very quiet drive home that day. As we were driving along the coastline, I looked at the waves and was lost in the thought of going for a swim, when David finally spoke.

'Janelle, if you make me have kids, I'll resent you forever!'

Okay, what? His sudden outburst resulted in a massive argument. I was in just as much shock as he was and this affected my life as well. *Did I want children? Could I love a child and not do to the precious child what my parents did to me? Would the child love me?*

I responded, 'If we did have a child, I wouldn't stay with you if it didn't work 'cause I would never want our child to live the life I did.'

Neither of us said much for a few days after that. The silence was broken after David got roaring drunk one night and exclaimed, 'Let's do it!'. I had no idea what he was on about. Then I worked it out and told him we'd wait until he'd sobered up and talk about it the following day. I went to bed feeling very overwhelmed, because I still had no idea what I wanted to do. This decision would change our lives in so many ways.

Usually, what David said while drinking was completely different the next day. The next day we were talking by the pool and I asked him if he remembered what he said to me.

'Yeah, I remember,' he said.

'Are you sure? Because I've been thinking, and this is massive. Do you even want kids, David? We haven't even spoken about them.'

'Yes, I want to be a dad one day. In my head, I figure you and I get along well and you want kids, I want kids, so why not?'

So that was that. We were going to try to have a baby!

I instantly went into cleansing mode. I wanted to heal the chain of command so that I would never parent my child the way my parents did me. I met with all sorts of holistic healers, went through past life cord cuttings, tried hypnotherapy, kinesiology, acupuncture and began to build yoga and guided spiritual meditations into my daily life. David thought some of the things I did were crazy, but he knew what it meant to me, so he let me go. He really wanted me to leave my job, as he could clearly see the effects of their negativity and how they bullied me. But I stuck it out.

By the time I felt my body and mind were ready to start this next phase, David's drinking had increased a lot. The resulting carelessness was causing problems and as I was no longer drinking and partying with him, we had started to lose our identity as a couple. Despite the warning signs, we kept going ahead.

The day was upon us to start the road to having a child. I had to undergo surgery to clean out all scar tissue in my reproductive organs caused by endometriosis. The day after my operation, they started pumping me full of fertility medication and I was so hopeful that it would all happen quickly for us. The doctor had placed a ticking clock above my head, and I was anxious to fall pregnant.

Cycle after cycle resulting in nothing. It was so much to deal with mentally, not to mention physically. I was sick all day every day and couldn't do much about it except try to keep strong and be positive.

We had undergone five cycles and my body was tired; I wanted to have a break. My doctor encouraged me to increase my fertility medication from two per day to five per day and I worried about whether I could do it. David had a 'she'll be right' attitude to it all and told me I'd be fine.

I reluctantly followed the plan, but I was so sick that I vomited around the clock, feeling drained and having to have scans every couple of days to find out when was the best time to have sex. Where was David? He wasn't with me. He was either drinking or fishing. I dragged him along to my next scan.

'The next three days is your window, so go have fun,' the specialist said. 'Wherever you are David, Janelle better be with you.'

'What do you mean, doc?' David replied. 'I was going fishing this weekend! Oh shit!'

I was furious at the flippant nature of the words that came out of his mouth.

'I have not taken these pills and undergone the surgery and changed my life to accommodate you going fishing! You said you wanted this, too!'

I cried the whole way home.

The thought of having sex when I was so upset just didn't excite me; there was no passionate connection. I did some research and there were certain positions we could try that didn't involve me looking at him. I made a joke out of giving some of those a try. Deep down, we both wanted a baby, but the pressures of it all were mounting and we just didn't know how to deal with it. We did as we were told and both hoped it was successful.

Now, the waiting game.

Ten days later, I had to leave work early to have blood tests. I returned to work with the knowledge I would be notified of the results by the end of the day. When I walked into the salon, one of my colleagues handed me a timer.

'Put it on for three hours and you aren't to look at your phone or answer the salon phone till then.'

Thankfully, I was so busy that afternoon that it wasn't a problem. I remember hearing the phone ring several times, but I couldn't answer it as I was so busy. Just as we were closing, I walked past the front desk and the phone rang. I answered and it was the specialist's office. *Am I pregnant?*

YES! Yes, I was. I ran into my boss' office thinking he'd be happy for my news, as he knew what I had been through. Instead, he cried and said, 'What about the salon? You didn't think of the salon, did you?'

Ah, excuse me? I grabbed my things and walked out. I wasn't letting him take this moment from me.

The following months were hard because I was so sick. The pregnancy drained me, but I continued to work the whole way to the end. I took eight weeks off as I had plenty of leave owed to me.

One morning I was so sick that I was laying in the bathtub. David was watching TV waiting for me, as we were going out for breakfast.

'Would you shut up and stop being sick?' he called out.

I was so emotional and tired, this harmless enough comment hurt so deeply. I guess it hurt because I felt I was making all the sacrifices. My career was beginning to reach amazing levels. I had been chosen to work with some of the leading national and international hair stylists and colourists of that time. I was making amazing money and hitting heaps of goals for myself both professionally and personally. Yet I was the one struggling to get out of bed every day and growing this beautiful baby inside me. I felt so alone. All of this was coupled with the fact I was super proud of my body and very grateful to be able to be pregnant.

I said all along this would probably be my only pregnancy, so I was going to buy the best of everything for this little person. I never wanted our child to feel second best and David understood that. When it came time to stop work, the staff put on a massive farewell event for me in the salon. I was overwhelmed with the love for me and my little baby. I read the card from my employers that night and it was the first time I felt appreciated in four years. I still have that card today.

I had trained my staff to take over the salon and my clientele to the best of my ability. I felt very confident in the future I had helped create for everyone, but now was time for me.

My sister was studying her finals in nursing and needed to do her final practical placement, so I said she could live with David and I while doing this. I figured the company would also be nice at home. David was always working, drinking or fishing, so I had a lot of time on my hands. I caught up with girlfriends and my parents visited now and then, but it just didn't feel right. I had a girlfriend who was a couple of weeks in front of me with her pregnancy, so we spent a lot of time together. My staffy, Zed, and I were extremely close so wherever I went, he came too.

The baby's room was coming together nicely, and I finally started to have a few good days where I had lots of energy and felt amazing. David started to slow down on the drinking as it was getting close to the due date and I was having heaps of Braxton Hicks contractions.

David went out fishing two weeks before our baby was due. He was only meant to go for a few hours, then it got dark and he couldn't be contacted, as he was out of mobile range. I called the partner of the friend he was out with and was freaked out to learn that she hadn't heard anything either and was extremely concerned. A few more hours passed and we still hadn't heard anything.

I called the coast guard, but the boat radio and signal box weren't working. I was at home alone, eight-and-a-half months pregnant while the father of my baby could possibly be lost at sea. Can you imagine what was going through an emotionally charged pregnant woman's mind?

About 7am my phone rang and it was David. I was so happy and asked if he was okay. He didn't seem to understand my distress at all, so my relief soon turned into anger and I told him to come home straight away. I had never done this before; usually I was very relaxed and went with the flow. But knowing he was about to become a father and was prepared to leave me for that length of time out of range just made me mad.

One week later, I gave birth to my darling daughter. My birth was extreme and quick, but we both did so well. We called her Maddison. Oh, what a sweetheart!

A Mother's Battle

When Maddison was four weeks old, I noticed her tummy was rather swollen. I mentioned it at mother's group and to a child nurse and they said it was normal to have some abdominal swelling from time to time. At her eight-week immunisations, she seemed okay. She had them at 8am that morning and at lunchtime I had to go to the supermarket. I lifted her out of her car seat, walked about twenty metres to an ATM and she let out a massive scream. I instantly felt hot liquid run down my leg. I rushed her to the mothers' rooms and my poor baby had bright lime green mess pouring out of her bottom; she also began to vomit.

Panic took over as I rushed her straight to the doctor. On examination, it was discovered she'd had a dangerous reaction to the rotavirus vaccine. We stayed in the doctors' rooms until we had her stabilised. She was very dehydrated and I wanted to take her to hospital, but David pushed for us to go home, arguing that we wouldn't get any sleep at the hospital and he had to work the next day.

Our doctor looked at me and asked if I thought I could handle that. I looked at David and he nodded his head. I was in so much shock I couldn't think straight, so I went along with David's decision. I had to feed Maddison with a dropper every ten minutes to keep her fluids up. She slept in my arms and I didn't sleep a wink. I started dozing off in the early hours, but woke to her crying again.

Ignoring the advice from the doctor, I listened to my gut, which was telling me that my baby was tired, sore and hungry. I tried to get her to attach to my breast and you know what? That beautiful little girl attached straight away. She was so frail and tiny, but her instinct for survival was strong. I only allowed a little at a time so as not to upset her stomach, but she eventually regained her hydration and was on the mend.

After this, she was just never the same. The doctor signed a form saying she didn't have to have the rest of her rotavirus vaccines, which was a relief, and he suggested I keep an eye on her. A few months passed and I noticed she kept struggling to pass a bowel motion and her sleep patterns changed. I went to the doctor again and was told the same thing: 'Just keep an eye on her.'

By six months it was getting worse, so a child health nurse suggested I start to give her solids, and instead of my breast milk, use formula. I wanted her to feel better, so I gave it a go and my angel didn't poo for a week. It was heartbreaking to see her in so much pain.

While all this was happening, David was putting the pressure on me to start back at work, so I made a few enquiries. I found an amazing day care for Maddie that understood my concerns for her health. I spoke to my old employer and they wanted me back – but on their terms. I was told if my baby was sick, I'd have to find someone else to look after her. I was at work to work, that I'd be paid at the senior stylist award rate, but be expected to be in charge of all staff training and daily running of the business.

'Thanks, but no thanks. My baby comes first,' I told them. It felt so liberating! During that meeting, they had told me that they only retained seventeen per cent of my clients. That meant the other eighty-three per cent were out there looking for a new hairdresser. I spoke to David and said if he wanted me to go back to work, I needed to be able to work from home.

So *Meek Hairdressing* was born.

Yay to independence! David would stop pressuring me and I could work around my daughter. This was going great as so many of my old clients returned. I had a single hairdressing station and chair set up in what once was my dining room. While that started off well, Maddie wasn't settling into day care life.

I had taken her to a few doctors. One had advised me to get her off my breast milk giving her goat's milk instead, and go gluten free with everything else. I had already tried going dairy free and gluten and wheat free myself to lower the amount in my breast milk and that didn't work, so I thought I'd give that a go as well. But because goat's milk didn't contain all the vitamins she needed, I had to add Pentavite to every bottle and she loved it. It was a small win and day care was now easier, but she still only went two days a week.

Her health started to get worse. Her bowel movements were like tiny rabbit poos and she struggled for hours to get them out. I started looking for other treatments for constipation. In the meantime, I was told I had to give her suppositories to help her have a motion. This was so hard and I felt horrible giving them to her the first time. I cried with her once I gave her the first dose and just held my little angel.

We worked with a naturopath and found out her bowel wasn't drawing in water – was a so-called dry bowel. We gave her herbal drops and worked with acupressure points. I even learned infant massage to help her. This did help a bit, but not a lot.

David had started studying a master builder's license three nights a week and we were doing renovations on the house to make more room and create more of a studio for me, as I was getting busier and busier.

I kept seeing the kinesiologist and I even had her do some balancing work on Maddison to release blockages. All this seemed to do was to just keep helping the surface issues and not the problem. I booked an appointment with a children's bowel specialist and was hopeful we might find a solution for her.

We started fertility treatment again as our specialist had advised, but David's drinking was getting out of hand. He couldn't deal with all the pressure and he chose to turn his back on all the emotional issues that he didn't want to face. His theory was if you don't know something, it's not your problem. The result was that he was doing what he wanted; fishing, drinking, studying, working and having his house cleaned, food cooked and clothes washed.

In contrast, I was undergoing fertility treatment, running the house, running my small business, caring for our daughter and doing all her medical treatment. David said to me one day if I wanted Maddie to have this treatment, I now had to pay for it all. I was so angry and disappointed. I said, 'Fine! I do it all anyway, so why not?' Clearly, we were really struggling as a couple.

It was time to persuade him to go for another fertility cycle. David was out drinking with a mate and I sent him a text saying, 'If we are going to do this, let's do it.' We had sex and then he went straight back out drinking, I remember laying there praying it worked, as I didn't want to do that again.

A few weeks later, Maddie became sick with tonsillitis and I was awake around the clock caring for her. In her dad's eyes, it was my job to care for her and I wasn't to wake him. He also told me I had to try and settle her quickly so he didn't wake. I was so tired and it was about 2am. I remembered I could do a pregnancy test that day so I went into the bathroom and took the test.

YES! I was pregnant! I was so excited I ran into David and woke him to tell him our news. His response was, 'Mmm. Great. I'm sleeping.' *Ahhh, men.* I was over this one-sided ruler bullshit.

A couple of weeks later, Maddie's bowels were the worst they had ever been. I was exhausted and fed up, so instead of taking her to her room so David didn't see it, I pulled out her portable change mat and sat on the floor doing my normal painful routine of suppository and tummy rub, lots of cuddles and watching her strain and scream. I had it down pat by now. I would put numbing cream around her bottom so if she tore, she didn't hurt. I made David watch what I had to do on a daily basis to make him understand why she needed help. It wasn't just me being over the top; there was something wrong. After I cleaned her up, he picked up his little girl with a tear in his eye and apologised to her and looked at me in sheer shock.

'I'm sorry I didn't listen, I'll do more to help,' he said.

We had an appointment with the specialist four weeks later. Maddie had to have scans and tests and be poked and prodded. As long as I was there, she was fine. Where was her dad though?

The specialist thought she had Hirschsprung's disease and said if the tests came back positive, a large portion of her bowel would have to be removed. There was a strong likelihood of her having to wear a poo bag for the rest of her life. I couldn't believe what I was hearing. I held my baby so tight knowing that within two weeks, he wanted to operate on her bowel.

I agreed to the surgery to take a small part of her intestines for testing. It was an anxious wait, but it was worth it. She didn't have that horrible disease. We were referred to an allergy paediatric specialist on the Gold Coast. She tested positive to dust mites, mould, smoke, cats, gluten, wheat, banana, corn and dairy. From here on in, we would follow a new diet and use allergy medications.

Something still wasn't right though. Her teeth were affected, her growth was affected and her diet had changed, yet her tummy was constantly swollen. She was always still smiling though. I was again very sick with my pregnancy. David and I were fighting heaps and I just wasn't happy.

I felt trapped and like the life was getting sucked out of me. We'd get along for about three days and after that we would have a fight. He would then say, 'Sorry, I understand, I'll do more,' yet nothing changed. Around November, I started to get bad cramps in my tummy, so I went to the doctor and they found out we were expecting twins, but one heartbeat wasn't as strong. They suggested I take it easy for a couple of weeks. *Pfft take it easy – how?*

Christmas was quickly approaching, and we were having a big Christmas lunch with David's family. I cooked a beautiful turkey with all the trimmings. I was opening the oven door to coat the turkey in juices again, when a sharp pain shot through my stomach. I dropped to my knees crying, desperately holding my tummy, praying I didn't lose the babies.

I crawled to the toilet. David was waiting for me when I came out, wanting to know what was happening.

'I'm bleeding, I think I'm miscarrying,' I said. 'I've got to get to the hospital.'

'Don't tell anyone,' he said. 'You go by yourself. We can't have you wreck Christmas Day. Maddie will be fine, just go.'

I was so worried about the babies that I didn't pause to consider what my partner had just said to me.

Once I got to Emergency, they put me on a heart monitor and did ultrasounds.

They found I had miscarried one of the babies and the other's heart was weak. I stayed in for a few hours till the bleeding eased. I got home in the early evening and told the family the sad news. I sat around for the next few days, trying to be positive for the baby who I thankfully was still carrying and for Maddie, my little princess.

It was my birthday and I wanted to take Maddie to Australia Zoo and have an elephant encounter. I remember walking into the zoo and feeling the need to go to the toilet, so I went to the bathroom but nothing but a trickle of urine came out. This was strange, as I felt I had a full bladder. I tried not to think too much about it, as I had been stressed enough and today was about family.

This kept happening all day and into the night and the next day it was worse. I kept working as I had a really busy day in my home salon. I dropped Maddie at day care and went straight home. I needed the toilet so badly that I ran inside, but this time nothing came out and the pain was excruciating. I started getting hot flushes and feeling panicked. My first client came and left and I was onto my second colour. My client took one look at me and said, 'Janelle, call your obstetrician now or I'll call him for you.' I spoke to the nurse in his clinic and she told me to head straight to the hospital and my obstetrician would meet me there.

I called David and he said, 'What do you want me to do? You have to find your own way there.' When Kelly heard him say this via loud speaker, she said, 'Janelle honey, that man's a dick. I'm taking you, let's go.' She took me to the private hospital and I met with my doctor. He immediately catheterised me to release the pressure and ran some tests.

The baby was stuck in my pelvis and not correctly positioned in the larger area in my uterus, so my urethra was cut off by the baby and my bladder nearly burst. This was a life-threatening situation. I was told I had to self-catheterise each time I had to go to the toilet and visit the obstetrician in his rooms to try and get the baby moved up every four days for the next eight weeks. I was to lay in downward dog position and do set exercises at the same time.

I called David to see if he could pick me up; he told me he was too busy at work. I called Beth and she picked me up and took me to buy all the medical supplies I needed. I picked up Maddie on our way through and by the time I got home, David was home drinking beers again.

He knew I was mad and disappointed in him when I didn't even say hi. Why waste my breath? All I said was, 'For the first couple of goes, I'll need your help to hold a mirror for me so I can see what I'm doing down there.' He agreed to help. I started to make dinner and then had to go to the toilet, so I called out to David and he came to the bathroom with me.

He could see how scared I was; trying to self-catheterise with a little belly was challenging. We got set up and David was holding the mirror, but all of a sudden, he dropped it into the toilet and said, 'Do it yourself, this is bullshit.' I screamed out for him to come back. I needed help. But he didn't come back.

Maddie walked around the corner saying, 'Mumma! Mumma!' I instantly found the courage I needed and I did it myself. *Fuck you, David. Fuck you.* I didn't speak to him much after that day. It was clear our relationship was in trouble. His controlling ways and the lack of emotional support, let alone some help at home, were wearing thin.

I did what the doctor said and we got to sixteen weeks gestation. He told me to make sure David was with me at the next appointment, which would be the last chance we'd have to try to move the baby up into my uterus. If it didn't work, we would have to terminate. That included surgery and I simply couldn't let myself think that was going to be the outcome.

I tried to express to David how badly I wanted him there with me. *Was I talking to a wall? Did I not speak clearly enough? Or was he just simply not open to hearing what I was saying?* I sat alone in the waiting room when the day came. I waited and waited. He knew what time he had to be there. My name was called and I had a sinking feeling in my stomach. *He isn't coming.* Then my phone went off. 'Sorry Janelle, I can't make it.'

I had no choice – it was me and me alone.

I climbed up on the table. This time, my legs were secured in leg supports and the nurse held my hand as silent tears were rolling down my face. I braced myself for whatever was meant to be. On pre-ultrasound, the baby's heart rate was extremely high and that was concerning before anything else had even happened.

It was all over in about fifty seconds, but feeling my baby be punched – and I mean literally punched – up out of my pelvis was beyond anything I could ever have imagined. Holy hell! I felt like my whole insides were pushed into my chest and the pain was so intense before the massive surge of adrenaline kicked in. *I hope that was it, because I never want to feel that again!* The doctor did an ultrasound straight away and it worked! The instant relief from hearing him say it was successful made me scream out with joy.

'So this means I keep my baby!' My elation was unlike anything I had ever experienced before. I asked to find out the gender, as I felt I hadn't bonded with this pregnancy like I had to my first because I was living in fear of losing it. The amazement of seeing my baby healthy and measuring a healthy size was enough, but when I found out it was a little boy it was the best feeling in the world.

I instantly named him after my Poppy, who to me was my hero. David and I had agreed on Jayden as the first name if we knew the baby was a boy. Despite my anger at him not being there, I was so excited to call David thinking he would be waiting by the phone. But he didn't even pick up. Without thinking, I called my dad. When I heard his voice, I burst into tears. 'You have a grandson dad; I'm having a boy!'

To this day, I ask myself why is it that I called my father when I was feeling so raw and emotional. I guess the truth is I just wanted to be loved by my father. He always wanted a grandson and out of seven grandchildren, Jayden is the only boy. I hoped he might be the connection that would finally bring me closer to my father and he would make that positive change.

◊

When Jayden was six months old, my close friend Rachel was turning thirty and had organised a get-together in Hervey Bay. I was so excited to attend, as Rachel was such a vibrant, bubbly woman who I looked up to. She had lost her sister in a horrific high-speed car accident, so having her closest family and friends there to celebrate with her was the perfect birthday wish.

I had been communicating with my parents and they had come to visit us a few times without any drama. I put this down to having a new baby boy to change the dynamics. David chose not to come to Hervey Bay with me as he'd rather go fishing, so it was decided that I would travel with the children and stay at my parents' house for two nights.

This made me nervous, but I agreed to trying.

All went well as I arrived and settled into mum and dad's place. The kids were happy when I left for the party, but I always had a sinking feeling in the pit of my stomach whenever my parents were involved in my life.

I sent numerous texts throughout the night to try to soothe my anxiety, but there was so much pressure from my friends at the party to just trust my parents. But they had no idea of the depth of the unhealthy relationship I had with my parents and dark thoughts swirled through my mind. *If he hurt my children or if mum plays the cover-up card and watches on as the darkness happens, I'll never forgive them and the pain I would want to cause to them both.* The anger I had in me was the manifestation of the abandonment I'd felt my whole life, the distrust, the sadness, the guilt, the shame the self-sabotage.

After a few hours, I excused myself from the party, which was filled with people having the best time. In the quiet of my car, a sinking feeling grew in the pit of my stomach the closer I got to my parents' house and I felt like I was carrying the weight of a small elephant as I pulled into the driveway. As I approached the front door, everything was quiet. As I stepped inside, I saw my dad sitting on the couch looking blanked-faced at the TV and my mother in the kitchen making a cup of tea. When mum returned to the living room, I asked how the kids were at bedtime. The look they exchanged only lasted a second, but it seemed to validate all of my worst fears.

'They both took a while to settle, but its okay now,' Mum said.

What does that mean? What isn't she telling me? Both the children were too little to verbally tell me if anything had happened. The mother guilt I had from leaving them with my parents gripped me with full force and I felt sick. No longer one to suppress what I think, I told my parents what was on my mind.

'I trusted you to look after my children. I said there would be none of your bullshit and you would treat them with love. If you haven't done that, I'm done with you.' They tried to reassure me that everything was fine, but there was just a chill in the air and I felt an unease around what they were holding back.

I went into my room, where Jayden was asleep in his cot and Maddie in my bed. I spent hours just watching them that night with my door closed and I took comfort in the knowledge that we would be leaving the next afternoon.

The next morning, both the children were extra cuddly with me, almost clingy. This did little to settle my unease. *Are they just picking up on my stress? Did something happen to them? Oh, how I wished they could talk to me and tell me!*

I had arranged to do Gran's hair while I was visiting, so I waited until I put both the children down for their midday nap before I snuck around the corner to Gran's house. I knew I had a few hours up my sleeve as they usually slept a while at that time of the day. Just as I was finishing her hair, I had a call from mum.

'Janelle, I need you to come home now.' It was all she said, but those eight words made my adrenaline level hit the roof.

Chapter 10

Cutting Ties

Oh my god, what had happened? I ran out the door without so much as a goodbye to Gran – there was no time to explain – and raced around the corner to find mum out the front with Maddie.

She was yelling out, 'Janelle! Janelle! I'm sorry!' as I pushed past her. I didn't know what was going on, but the fact that I couldn't see my boy or my father made it easy to put two and two together to realise my worst fear was now playing out in front of me.

'What the fuck, Anna! I'll kill him! You know I will!' I shouted as I bolted through the front door.

I could hear banging coming from my bedroom, like the walls were being smashed, followed by the unmistakable sound of my six-month-old baby boy screaming. *If he's hurt my son, he won't get back up,* I seethed as I sprinted down the hallway. I swung open the door to find my dad in full rage, dazed, confused, muttering nonsense words repeatedly while aggressively punching the walls. He looked like he was completely out of it, yet his body was in full motion. I'd seen that look from him many a time. It was a look that tortured my soul. I pushed him out of the way and picked up my baby boy, who was unharmed physically, but clearly distressed. I could hear mum already trying to justify the scene in front of me.

'Your dad doesn't mean it. He was just laying down with Jayden for a rest. He doesn't mean it Janelle,' she pleaded as I put Jayden down in the living room, but I was not going to listen this time.

I followed my dad down the hallway and pushed him up against the wall in the kitchen. A red-hot anger washed over me and I punched him. I punched him again, and I felt a full embodiment of revenge, protection, bravery and anger. He fell to the ground, never once hitting me back. He lay there just taking my beating, but his surrender did little to soften my rage. I started kicking him in his back with all my strength, with no care whatsoever for the damage I could be inflicting. The little girl in me who was beaten repeatedly and manipulated and shamed and abandoned by him just needed to release the pain inside.

My mother was trying to pull me away, but I had a next-level strength, like a powerful force had been unleashed. When I stopped, he crawled to his room crying without a word or so much as a glance in my direction. He slammed his bedroom door then a few minutes later, I could hear him bashing his fists against the wall once again. My mother screamed for me to help him.

'Why the fuck is it up to me to stop him? He's your husband, you sort him out!' I yelled back. She was so scared of him; I could see it in her eyes. *Was this why she never stepped in front of his fist as he used to beat me as I child? What had happened to her? Why was she such a coward?* I pushed her to take responsibility as I focused on packing up our things. We were going to leave and never return. Knowing I was not going to assist in any way, mum gingerly let herself into the room with dad and things appeared to settle for a spell. The unmistakable sound of smashing glass permeated through the walls and mum screamed out for me.

'Your father's kicked through the shower screen! He says he's going to cut his throat!' I didn't respond. I'd checked out. I didn't care.

Let him do it if he wants to.

With everything packed, the house was still once more, and I was just about to leave with the children when mum came running out and grabbed my arm. '

Janelle! Janelle, your dad just keeps asking for you. Please go talk to him. He's in bed now. He's calmed down.' I don't know why I was compelled to follow her request, but I softened and walked to his room.

I vividly remember stepping into his room and seeing him in bed, looking like a broken man, as tears streamed down his face. On his bedside table was a cross-stitch I had made for him when I was very little. It depicted a man in a hospital bed with a heart chart being displayed on the foot of the bed and a nurse standing near. I'd had it framed and written a note saying, 'I Love You Dad'. I felt an overwhelming sadness and saw that he was trapped in a body of pain. He did love me, but the demons inside him were stronger than his love for me. He hated what he had done, but once the shadows inside him took hold, everything went dark.

'Gubby, I'm sorry, I'm so sorry,' he said. Once the tears stopped, he was able to gather himself and continued. 'Those other cunts never tried to stop me, I'm sorry. When I asked who he meant, he replied, 'Your mother, Alice and Emily. They just let me go. I couldn't stop myself girl, I'm sorry. I hate them for it. I love you Gubby.' He actually wanted someone to stop him, but no one ever did. The realisation was powerful for me, but it didn't change a thing. He was completely out of control, and I was no longer going to put myself or my children in harm's way.

As he often did after the intensity of an episode, dad fell asleep. I went back to the children thinking, *oh my God what have they just seen? How is this going to affect their lives? I made a promise when I became their mother, to never let them see this sort of life.*

I was surprised to find my two nieces in the living room. Mum told me while I'd been in with Dad, she had called Emily to come over to say goodbye.

'Where is Emily?' I asked when I couldn't see my sister anywhere.

'She's gone in to see Dad....'

'Why the hell would you send her in there? He was sleeping! Don't wake him, he'll get worse!'

I knew it would be too late for me to stop her, so I jumped to my feet and was quickly trying to get all the kids out of the house.

The inevitable happened and dad stormed out of his room in full rage again. This time, he was consumed with an intensity of darkness I hadn't seen before. I called out for my oldest niece to run to me, but he was in between us and put his arm out and coat-hangered her. She landed with a sickening thud on her back, and I rushed forward to pick her up and carried her out to my car, where the other children were already gathered.

Mum and Emily came running out behind me, closing the door behind them. Emily was pale and was apologising profusely. Mum was crying again, and I had to step up once more and be the strong one for the whole family. Dad was swearing at the top of his lungs, one word after another in a constant stream and we could hear holes being punched into the walls again. We waited for the lull, but this time it seemed it wasn't going to stop.

Knowing this was well beyond our ability to control, Mum, Emily and I agreed to call the police. We used my phone to call them on loudspeaker, with all of us giving information to the first response operator. We could hear the sirens within minutes and a paddy wagon, a standard police car and an ambulance pulled into the driveway. The officers had also called in the dog squad in case dad made a run for it and were equipped with taser guns.

I remember looking back at my dad at the doorway when the police stormed the house and were bringing him out to the paddy wagon. He had both arms reached out over the officer's shoulders, yelling out for me. Telling me he loved me.... As I got in the car and drove down the street, another police car pulled up alongside me. I put my window down and spoke to the officer. He asked where I was going and if it was going to be safe. I said I would take the kids to my sister's house for the night and leave the next morning. He took all my details and we drove off. As shocked as I was by the events that had just unfolded, I had to control my desire to curl up in a corner and shake the fear out of me. For the sake of the kids, I pushed it down and did my best to create a sense of security for them.

I fed the kids, bathed them and gave lots of cuddles, especially to my niece who had been hurt. I spoke to her about it and reminded her that she was safe and I'd never let anyone hurt her. I would protect all of them, always. Emily called me and checked in on how the children and I were doing. When she heard we were all okay, she told me she and mum had called the family and let them know what had happened. I was surprised by this, because the usual run of events would see them brush this under the carpet and pretend like nothing had ever happened. I didn't think anything of it at the time, instead asking after dad. She told me the police had arrested him and taken him to the lock-up at the police station.

She said she'd come back home, so I could go and get my things from my parents' house while he wasn't around. I hadn't given much thought to the bags we'd abandoned in our rush to get out of the house, so I agreed that was a good idea. I had put all the kids to bed and night fell before Emily came back, so there was another ominous level added to the situation as I got into the car to drive back to my parents' home in the dark. The trip was so raw and emotional, as I imagined what would happen when I arrived. *What will I say to my mother? What would she say to me? How did my life get to this point? What sort of messed up family am I a part of? They just keep sweeping the truth away and telling lies to cover up how broken we are.*

The air felt heavy as I stepped into the house, as if the walls were still carrying the trauma and sadness of the day's events.

Not wanting to spend a second longer than necessary in there, I walked straight to my room to collect my bags. But as I turned around to leave, I saw her, that weak excuse of a mother. She put me in the firing line and allowed me to cop the abuse while she just cried and said, 'Please stop.' She grabbed my arm and started the fake tears again. All I could think about were all the times when she had put me in the firing line. My father's words were ringing in my ears: *I wanted them to stop me... they just let me go.* 'Anna your crocodile tears don't work on me anymore. What sort of mother are you?'

I had finally asked her the question that had been eating me up inside since I was a child. I couldn't stand the sight of her any longer and tried to walk past her, but she refused to budge.

I pushed her against the linen cupboard.

'Let me ask you something. Was I that bad of a child that you seriously think it was okay to tell people I was so naughty that you and dad lost control of me? That I was the cause of all the family problems? You had three daughters, Anna. The youngest used drugs at fourteen and was pregnant at seventeen, the middle child stole from you time and time again and was violent. Then there was me, who just thought, *Fuck it! I must be all these bad things if I'm getting treated this way.* You, mum, brainwashed me, manipulated my thoughts and memories to create a story that wasn't true!' I was on a roll now and felt like I had to get it all off my chest.

'You took my innocence and made me out to be a troublemaker. All I ever wanted was to be loved and feel safe! TELL ME ANNA! TELL ME... WAS I THAT BAD? DO YOU THINK WHAT YOU ALL DID WAS RIGHT? I was molested by a school dentist and instead of you being there for me, you dropped me at Nanna's house and never spoke of it again. What sort of mother are you? You overcompensate with Alice and Emily, but stand by and watch me get hurt over and over again!'

Mum fell into the chair by the telephone on the wall in the kitchen. Her head dropped into her hands and she sobbed. 'No Janelle. No, you were never bad and I'm sorry!'

With that being said, I walked out of the house and headed back to Emily's.

◊

On the drive back, I felt my heart break into a million fragments. I didn't know how to process so much confrontation in such a short space of time, so instead my natural instincts kicked in and I stepped into the protective warrior version of me. It was comfortable, like a second skin I would wear that allowed me to channel my intense emotions and fight the fights I had to, to protect myself and the ones I loved the most.

When I walked into Emily's house, she asked me to call Alice before leaving to go back to mum's house. She wanted to be there until we knew what was happening with dad.

I hesitantly dialled her number. Alice was a nurse and lived on the Gold Coast. She always came across to me as if she knew everything and that she could control any situation, even at a distance. We had a past filled with anxiety, aggression, competitiveness and sibling rivalry.

I was filled with dread as the dial tone rang. Before I could even take a breath, the abuse began.

'Why didn't you call me? I would've been able to talk sense into dad! Look what you've done, Janelle! You've made a big mistake in calling the police. Mum and Emily have called everyone in the family and we are all blaming you. You made the call to the police. It's always been you to cause pain in the family.' This continued for several minutes before it all became too much and I snapped, raising my voice.

'ALICE! Stop! Shut up and listen... Dad was not stopping. You weren't there Alice, you can't blame me. Mum, Emily and I called the police together thanks, it wasn't just me! And what do you mean they've called all the family?'

Ignoring my question, Alice went on and on about how she could save dad.

I began to notice messages and missed calls coming in from my aunties, from my dad's mother and from cousins.

All blaming me.

Only hours before, I had been doing my Gran's hair and connecting through conversation. Now, Gran said I was dead to her and she never wanted to speak my name out loud ever again. The other messages held similar sentiments; I wasn't in the family anymore, they wanted me gone. All to cover up the truth of the monster they all enabled and protected.

◊

In my heart, mind and soul, I knew I was different to them all. I knew the truth and I held onto that, not just to survive, but to find the strength to make sure I never lived through this sort of abuse ever again.

I was alone again, and this time it was final.

At the first sign of day breaking, I woke my children up and drove away. This was life changing for me, and I would never be the same ever again. The trauma from the event was starting to take a hold of me. The shadows were gripping onto me, and I so desperately wanted to break free. David's parents' house was only a few kilometres out of town, so I called David and said I would be stopping at their place because I couldn't focus on driving, I was far too distressed.

When I got to Joseph and Evelyn's house, I fell out of the car into Joseph's arms while Evelyn walked the kids into the house. I was completely broken, my heart shattered. My soul had been to such a low, dark vibration I didn't know how I would get back up. It was as if the shadow that haunted my existence had overwhelmed my entire body and I felt like all love was drained out of me.

While Maddison played and I breastfed my sweet six-month-old baby boy, I cried such sad tears of letting go of the life I had lived. I knew I had to now focus my energy on figuring out where to go next. Once I had rested and got my thoughts clear, I continued the drive home.

I am forever grateful for the openness from Joseph and Evelyn. Their love and support that day meant I could hold faith in trusting others. To have support at my darkest soul-shattering moment was invaluable. I felt so much blame and shame. If I didn't go back, if I had listened to my inner voice, none of this would've happened. I wouldn't have felt that intense pain and exposed my children to that darkness within my family.

On top of all of that, the people I had called my family my whole life now had turned their backs on me in light of the lies told by my mother and younger sister to protect the darkness within the walls of the house of shadows.

All these thoughts flooded my mind and played with me the entire two-and-a-half hour drive home. The children slept the whole time, leaving me alone with my mind. I had time to think, time to breath, and the one constant thought was, *I promise my babies – Mumma will never let these people hurt you, I commit to giving you both the best life I can possibly give.* Once I landed on this, I repeated it almost in a chant to not only tell them, but to make a promise to myself.

By the time I got home, David was waiting for me with worry etched into his face. He was so sad for me and also so mad that they would do what they did. He also felt some guilt that he didn't come with me. Would they have done what they did, if he had? I will never know.

I spent the next few months on a deep journey within. I focused on setting myself free from the trauma. I spent time asking myself what made me happy. What do I need? Who do I feel I can trust? I went to a Cognitive Behavioural Therapy (CBT) therapist, who taught me ways to not only understand my pain, but to heal the shadows that I was so scared of. I did this because I finally began to understand my 'why'. Why I hurt. Why I tried to keep a connection with my dad after all he'd done to me. Why I was still so scared.

Having this time of peace and freedom to focus on myself and begin to understand what was driving my actions, reactions and thoughts, I began to feel more like myself again. I liked who I was. I believed in myself. I knew I could build a better future.

The peace I felt during that journey was short-lived, as I began to receive many missed calls from my parents and sisters. I didn't answer any of them. Then David answered his phone one evening and yelled out to me, 'Janelle, it's your mum. You need to talk to her.' It was the last thing I wanted to do, but I took the call. Her voice was panicked.

'Janelle, from the situation that happened, your dad was police ordered to have a psychiatric assessment and a full health check.

He has a form of schizophrenia and a rare type of thyroid cancer and needs immediate surgery.'

They always exaggerated everything, so I was immediately suspicious. *Is this just some sick mind game they are playing to suck me back in again? Or is this the truth? If it was, did I really give a damn? If this is his path, let him go. If this is his suffering, it's his, not mine. I'm not going to be a victim of their darkness ever again. I love myself more...* 'Anna... is he going to die?' The question caught her off guard and she didn't respond.

'I don't care anymore. Stop with the games. Just let me know if he lives or dies.' With that, I ended the call.

David looked at me with his eyebrows raised, wanting to know what had just happened, but I grabbed my sneakers and said, 'I have to go for a run. I'll call you while I'm running to fill you in.'

And off I went. Running was such a release for me and I knew I needed the adrenaline that ran through me, which was similar to the fight or flight high that I knew all too well. I had to keep reminding myself that I was safe. I was in no danger and I had control, to not let myself be drawn back into their darkness.

After I had exhausted my nervous system, I stopped and called David to let him know what my mother had said.

'Janelle, you know what they are like. You have to do what's best for you. What do you want to do? Do you want them in your life?' I answered quickly: 'NO!'

At that point, the thought of my father dying didn't upset me at all. I was numb to any emotion regarding him, like I could feel everything but nothing at the same time. I was trying to explore the depths of my inner self, the innocence of my childhood that had been tainted by their filth, their drama, their control, and their lies.

I made the decision that I didn't want to know. I didn't want to know them or anything that came with them.

I wanted to be free.

As they chose to turn the family against me, so I walked away from them all and have never looked back. It was the most important decision I've ever made and I honour that decision with every cell of my body.

Chapter 11

Out of the Blue

Days turned into weeks, weeks into months, months into years and I focused on my own family and building us up to be the family I wished I'd always had. We were happy, healthy and I was in a good place emotionally after working on myself for a few years. Sitting at traffic lights on a beautiful Sunday afternoon, I was returning home from buying my son his birthday presents for his second birthday, which was in ten days. With a contented love for my babies and the fresh outlook I now had for my life, I was on a call to a friend of mine talking about how I felt I was drifting away from David. We were becoming two completely different people; I felt he was draining me and I could see that our relationship only existed because of the children.

'You have to do what will make you happy,' she said in one of her pep talks that always made me feel better. 'Please don't stay with someone just because of the children. I believe you can find your happiness you are so deserving of.' I had stopped at the traffic lights along Nicklin Way in Kawana, facing north, when I saw a red Holden Commodore speeding in the opposite direction. I instantly had a thought that I was in danger. It came out of nowhere. As I instinctively gripped the steering wheel, I heard: *Hang on, you'll be okay. Just hang on.* A cold shiver ran down my spine as the lights turned green.

I checked my mirrors and saw the same red car racing up behind me, showing no signs of slowing down. I turned my head to look over my left shoulder, wanting to make sure what I had seen was real. Before I could look forward again, BANG! My car was slammed through the intersection and all I could hear was a gut-wrenching sound of metal on metal as the red car side-swiped the length of the left-hand side of my car. With my soul feeling as if it was getting ripped out of my body, I saw a vision of my children before I felt an eerie calm come over me. A sense of nothingness. *Where is this space? Where were my children? Why can I see my body?*

It seemed like forever, but at the same time only an instant, before a sudden jerk brought me back into my body. I could see my hands still gripped on the steering wheel and when I looked up, I saw the red car sideways between two trees in the middle of the road.

Why isn't my body moving? What is all this pain? I was frozen in place, but acutely aware of smoke starting to come from the red car. I still to this day have no memory of how I got myself out of my car. The forensic police report states: 'Female driver removed herself from vehicle before roadside seizure occurred.'

All I remember was screaming out the names of my children before finding myself on the road, lying by the driver's side rear tyre, watching fire crew spray my car with a green foam.

A man and his son placed a towel over my body to keep me warm as people ran and yelled around us. I heard a loud *thud* followed by swearing as various ambulance paramedics, police officers and firemen called out to one another and scattered. I saw a guy running to the right of me and someone chasing after him before tackling him and slamming him to the ground. I found out later this was the driver of the car that hit me. Before I had time to register much else, my body was being lifted into the back of an ambulance. My mobile was still clenched in my hand and was ringing. I had subconsciously started to organise someone to look after the kids so David could come to hospital. *How am I doing this?* I marvelled as I became conscious once again of my action. I didn't even know what had just happened – I hadn't even seen the injuries my body sustained – but all I wanted to do was look after my children and fight to see them again.

I was taken to hospital, with the Commodore driver in a separate ambulance. My next memory is seeing police running all over Emergency at Caloundra Hospital and into a private room, while I lay in a full body spinal brace in the corridor, urgently needing the toilet. I was crying and frozen by the pain and shock my body was in. I kept asking for help but was dismissed, as the male driver that hit me was extremely violent and causing a scene. The hospital was understaffed, and I was told I'd have to just pass my bodily fluids and they'd clean me up. *How humiliating! Why am I not being looked after?*

I passed out again as my body was seized by a fresh round of shock. The next time I opened my eyes, David was next to me and I was in a private room dressed in a hospital gown. I was being told all sorts of things from David and hospital staff, as well as having police in my room asking questions. I was dazed and confused in the flurry of activity and was whisked in and out of the room to go for scans and X-rays. They had wanted me to go for an MRI, but the machine operator had already left for the day, so they discharged me with strict instructions to visit my GP the next morning. While we were on our way home, David declared he was hungry and decided to head into the Hungry Jacks drive-through.

Crying out in pain every time he hit the speed bumps on his way, I remember looking at him knowing our relationship was done. *What a heartless thing to do! How could he be thinking of his stomach at a time like this? He really mustn't care.* I didn't sleep a wink that night, the pain was increasing and was so blinding I honestly thought I could die from the agony.

David took me to the doctor first thing in the morning as per the instructions from the hospital, but he didn't even walk me in. He just dropped me off and went away to do other things.

My doctor was shocked by the state of me and asked what had happened. As soon as I finished explaining, his face was pale.

'I stopped at the scene of the accident after the ambulance had taken you to hospital as I was driving to visit my mother,' he said. 'Why are you here? Why aren't you still in hospital?'

'They said they didn't have the right staff on to conduct my MRI and I should come here.'

He picked up the phone and dialled the ambulance and I was rushed off to the Private Hospital to have all the correct scans. The results were beyond anything I could have imagined. I had a prolapsed C3, C4, C5, C6 and T1, tears in my left brachial plexus and stage 2 impingement in my left rotator cuff.

The tests I had to undergo to determine the severity of my injuries were so painful and the first round of radical radio frequency treatment commenced. The spine is made up of twenty-four bones stacked into a column and between each vertebrae is a cushion – the disc – that acts as a shock absorber. There is also a facet joint, which allows the spine to twist from side to side and nerves come out from this. The nerves carry pain signals and allow responses of movement and sensation. Radio frequency ablation uses radio waves to create heat that is used to kill tissue. During the procedure, I had to be awake so they could check they got the correct placement, but also to assure I didn't become paralysed. It was a terrifying experience given how high the stakes were if something were to go wrong.

The loss of movement and the fear I had for my future were nothing compared to the fact I couldn't even cuddle my babies. They would have to be gently placed next to me on the couch and hold only my right hand, as they were so scared to touch me.

I was put on a crazy mixture of drugs for the pain: Lyrica, amitriptyline, diazepam, Kapanol, morphine, Endone, Norspan and Tramadol in large amounts. As I was unable to juggle them all, David and his mother were responsible for my medications. I kept saying I wanted my children, but Evelyn took it upon herself to tell me I was unfit and that they were her babies for now.

'I know what they need Janelle, just lay there and be grateful we are here to help.'

I was grateful, but my children were my everything, and I needed to be near them as much as possible, not separated from them. She did help a lot, but I saw another side to Evelyn during this time. David and his mother heavily restricted my time with the children and David told me my injuries were all in my head and I needed to get back to work, because he was sick of paying for me. It became clear he wanted me to look a certain way and be what he wanted me to be.

My blood pressure would drop suddenly when I would stand up, due to all the medications I was taking and I couldn't even tell if they were giving me the right doses. I was struggling so much.

All I wanted was to be better and to be with my children. Instead, I felt trapped, not only within my injured body, but trapped in my room by David and his mum while they kept the two most important reasons for my survival – my reason to fight, my everything – away from me. I expressed my stress to my dearest friends when they visited me.

They were starting to get worried about me, as they could see my spirit breaking and eventually decided to intervene.

Sue, a very special friend of mine who in a lot of ways was like a mother figure to me, was the first to step forward and help me gain my first steps towards my light. Sue would come over late every afternoon to help me have precious time with my little ones. She would place them in my arms with a warm bowl of popcorn on my chest and we would watch a movie as she sat in a chair in the corner of the room to make sure no one took that time away from us. Through this simple act of kindness, my mental strength started to grow.

My light, which had been dimmed by the medications I was given, started to shine again as I hid the pills and told Evelyn and David I had taken them. I knew I needed mental clarity, so I chose to feel the physical pain. I used the pain and taught myself how to harness it to drive me to get stronger. I had a second spinal radio frequency treatment not only on my neck, but also my shoulder, as nerve conduction tests came back with sixty-two per cent paralysis in my left arm. My specialist told me the orthopaedic surgeon wouldn't operate on my shoulder with the complexity of my injuries, so I had to learn how to live with what was, and try to regain as much strength as I could.

After months and months of healing on my own, I was given an opportunity to attend a rehabilitation program. This news gave me more hope than I ever had to regain a new life for myself and my children. We had just bought a new car, as the Toyota Prado I'd been driving at the time of the crash was a complete write-off. We chose another Toyota Prado as the forensic police said if I had been in anything smaller, I would've died on impact. With that in mind I will never feel safe in anything other than a four-wheel-drive.

David was nowhere near as excited as I was by the idea of the rehab program. In fact, he said if I wanted to go, I would have to drive myself. In order to do this, I had to not only learn how to drive again with one functioning arm, I had to overcome huge amounts of emotional trauma. Determined not to miss the opportunity to shift the trajectory of my life, I created my own desensitisation process.

To start, I sat in the back seat of the car with it parked securely within the fenced yard. I then asked for the car to be parked out on the footpath. The first day I did this, David was with Joseph, who had such a beautiful soul and really wanted me to regain my independence. He sat with me and I asked him to start the car whilst I was sitting inside. My heart was beating so fast in my fragile, healing body that I had to ask him to turn it off after only a few seconds.

The next day, we did it again and continued until I felt determined to sit in the driver's seat with the car running – it happened within a week. Each day I would meditate and focus on what I wanted to do, feel and to achieve. The Saturday when I started the car by myself, I felt such an overwhelming sense of pride. David took my positivity as a sign I was better, and I should be working again. When I told him I was nowhere near ready, he responded with: 'What is your problem? Enough is enough Janelle!' He had absolutely no idea of the level of pain I was in and how much strength, focus and energy it took just to get my mind willing to push my body to do such a simple action as to walk to my car, open the door, sit behind the wheel and start the engine. *Why can't he just be proud of me for what I am doing?*

I started seeing a PTSD psychologist named Tegan. She was such a blessing because the trauma was so deep within my soul that I could never have begun to work on it on my own. Tegan affirmed all of the work I had already done on my personal development and physical healing. She said they would become self-guiding tools for me in any situation I would face in my life. She also took me through a treatment that re-exposed me to triggers in relation to the car accident, which strengthened my ability to process and move forward from the trauma. I still have triggers to this day, but I have the universal tools of life that I've collected throughout my journey that I can call upon to help me in any situation.

David was asked to have a session with Tegan. Unbeknownst to me at the time, she had already sensed that he was a big block in my recovery on a mental and spiritual level.

Following David's assessment, he was diagnosed with emotional retardedness – look it up, it's a real condition – and it was such a turning point for me. I could so clearly see the patterns that were always there that had pulled us apart even before we had children. I had felt like I was dealing with the impacts of this accident completely alone and I really was. David had emotionally checked out, but it was not his fault; it was just how he was wired.

We were so different, yet I had become a co-dependent female since the accident. I struggled to dress myself, let alone run my hair studio from home. I didn't think I had a choice for a while there, but then my soul gave me a big push, just as it had many times already in my life. Those shadows from my childhood reminded me just how strong I was and that my purpose in life was to keep the promise I made myself so many years earlier – to never settle for anything or anyone of a negative character.

David was a good man, we just weren't good together. He wanted things a certain way because of his own upbringing. The shadows of his past weren't mine and mine weren't his. We started to argue more and more, and he had complete financial control. I would say things like, 'When I'm strong enough, I'm leaving. I said to you years ago David, I wouldn't stay in a loveless relationship just because we had children.'

I wanted better for my Maddison and Jayden. I'd rather have two happy homes rather than keep them locked in one that was becoming more and more toxic.

I had a specialised attachment added to my car so I could drive. It kind of looked like a doorknob and it allowed me to grip onto it with my right hand and turn corners. I also had driving cameras installed so I had complete visibility without blind spots, as I had very little movement range in my neck at that stage. With everything in place, I finally felt ready to attempt to drive the car.

The day I decided to brave the road, Maddie said, 'Mumma I'm coming too!' I looked at her sweet little face and I knew if she was in the car, I would have more focus on not giving into my fears of driving again. After all, she and her brother were my inspiration to get better.

As David put Maddie in her car seat for me and I placed my seatbelt on and turned the key in the ignition, I felt my whole world flash in front of me. But I didn't let fear hold me back.

I gripped the steering wheel and pulled onto the road. Oh my God, emotions were overwhelming as I pushed the accelerator pedal down ever so slightly. My pulse was racing, my palms were sweaty, and my eyes were dashing from the road in front to vision from all of the cameras to make sure I knew where everything was at every moment. I just drove around the corner and straight home. I kept saying, 'I did it Maddie! I did it!' Her beautiful little voice replied, 'Yay! Go Mummy, yay!' as she clapped her hands and giggled as though she understood the significance of what just happened. I hadn't seen any cars on the road, so it was a very gentle way of re-exposing myself to driving again.

I was booked in to start rehabilitation two weeks later and David doubled down on the fact I'd have to get myself there. At the time, I was so mad with him for saying that, but now I see that he just kept pushing me. I don't know where it came from within his heart, but I felt he was pushing me away, not pushing me to get better.

The next time I was behind the wheel, I drove around Coolum. My knuckles were white from holding on so tight and my mouth so dry I couldn't swallow. I don't even remember breathing. With the PTSD therapy I was doing, I was encouraged to drive through the intersection of the accident to re-expose myself, instead of holding fear and avoidance to it.

I sat with the idea for some time before I woke up one morning with a single thought: *I'm going today*. Again, Maddie came with me. I was so frightened that as I got closer, I kept singing with her and talking to her to distract me from what I was doing. It worked so well that I ended up in Caloundra – an extra fifteen minutes' drive away from the fateful intersection. When I realised where I was, I cried at the thought of the long drive back home.

As I approached the intersection on Nicklin Way on the way home, I really wasn't feeling very good at all. I kept praying the lights were green so I could just drive through. I couldn't cope with being stopped at a red light at the same intersection. As I was driving towards the intersection, I saw, to my horror, the lights changed to orange and then red. *No, no, no!* I called David crying, but he was not much help, 'Well, you have to get home somehow. Just keep driving.' As I ended the call, the lights turned green *Thank you universe.*

I don't remember the rest of the drive home, but I know I couldn't stand when I got out of the car. My entire body was shaking uncontrollably, and I had to wobble my way to my bedroom to lay down and allow the shock to wear off. As I lay there alone, I thought of all the ups and downs of my life, all the tests of my spirit and my inner belief and realised *I want more from my life. I have found the inner strength I needed many times over in the past, what is so different this time?* The stronger my mind and spirit became, the more David would try and control me. To rebel against this oppression, I would make myself stronger so I could fight back. I wasn't quite sure what to do with this realisation just yet, so I put a pin in it.

As the morning of the first day of rehab arrived, I felt equally nervous and excited, so much so that I could feel the blood pumping through my body. I kissed my babies goodbye and said, 'Mumma is going to get better, I promise. I'll pick you both up in my arms again.' With tears rolling down my face, I drove off to the one opportunity I had to get stronger and learn how to use my new body. There were different areas of the rehab course, which had a team made up with of an exercise physiologist, an occupational therapist, physiotherapist and psychologist.

Everyone attending had to have their injuries assessed. I was the only one with what was called a 'complexed injury,' meaning multiple areas of injury. I also was the only one with an upper spinal, shoulder and arm injury. In that first session, I was taught the basics of how to tie a shoelace, how to dress myself and how to cut up my own food, just for starters.

A few days in was the first time we had hydrotherapy. I trusted in my exercise physiologist, as he was responsible for my strength training and mobility, however that day he had to leave early and a female instructor took over the session. I was so determined to regain mobility, I trusted that she was briefed on my situation and would take the same level of care. All of a sudden, she had me doing a head turning exercise where I was submerged to my chin in the pool and I was told to turn my head right for six sets of ten and then to the left the same amount. I had no rotation to my left, so she demanded I do as much as I could with no excuses. I had to stop as I started to lose feeling in my body.

When I went to the toilets to get changed out of my swimmers, I felt a hot sharp pain shooting from my neck down to my feet. The next thing I remember was being on the floor in a full body spasm. My arm and neck were locked in an unnatural way and I was in so much shock, I couldn't even scream. I kicked the wall with my legs, hoping someone would hear me, as I was the only female in the pool that day besides the fill-in instructor; no one would be coming anytime soon. I was found by two male nurses, who had to cut my swimmers off me and put me in a full body brace until the spasm stopped.

I waited till I felt able to drive home again. I was determined to never be in that situation ever again. Just trusting in the medical staff to know what to do wasn't enough anymore. I started asking questions about everything they were teaching me and getting me to do. I was absorbing every bit of knowledge I could regarding my injuries and how to hopefully improve until I reached my goal of lifting my children into my arms.

My next appointment was with the physiologist, an older lady named Wendy, who was used to controlling her environment and the patients she treated. When I was vulnerable and a 'yes' person, she was pleasant and accommodating. But the moment I started asking lots of questions when something didn't fit in with my beliefs and goals, or I felt the techniques were outdated and asked for further clarification on why we were doing certain things, she became a different person.

I'm someone who doesn't get stuck in a low level of energy. I have always been given guidance from a deep place within me and that gut instinct is what has been my life's compass.

Wendy made it very clear she didn't like my questions and said by asking them, I was interfering with the program she had been doing for years and years. Who was I to challenge her on that? After my session with Wendy, I moved onto the next session with the occupational therapist, who taught me how to use a specialised cutting board so I could use my foot to cut tough food, and how to vacuum the floors with a specialised vacuum that wrapped around my waist. We were interrupted by Wendy, who asked if she could have a meeting with me afterwards.

I went to her office door feeling drained and she asked me to sit down.

'Something has come to my attention that is a concern to me,' she began.

Wendy said she felt my approach to my recovery was too aggressive and her program shouldn't be challenged by her clients. I reminded her of the severity of the incident with the instructor who hadn't been passed on the right information for me and how that had resulted in me spasming in a body brace.

'It's no wonder that I would lose trust in your so-called program,' I said. 'It is my body after all. I just want to understand the information I am being given.'

I had barely finished when she interrupted me and said, 'This Janelle, this is exactly what I am talking about. We are all trained professionals and by you questioning me, you are undermining myself and my program, not only in a one-on-one session, but also in group sessions.' She was clearly not hearing me, nor respecting my wishes. I left crying my eyes out, incredibly hurt by being told my approach to my recovery was 'too aggressive'. All I wanted to do was get better, to be the best version of myself and not settle for the diagnosis I had been labelled with. I wanted to move my body again, to regain functionality, and to move on and live life.

I filed a complaint and received approval to skip her sessions for the rest of the program.

On completion of the program, I was told what exercise equipment I needed at home to continue with my recovery. David and I bought what was needed and I did the work and was getting stronger every day, mentally and physically. David didn't like this. He already knew we were done and it was only a matter of time now. One night we had a massive argument resulting in him saying, 'You go Janelle, you go alone. You lose everything.' I called my closet friend, Livia, who was like a sister to me. 'Enough is enough Janelle. Just leave honey, let him take what he wants. We'll help you and the kids out.'

With that reassurance, I found a unit to rent and told David I was leaving. It had been fifteen months since the accident and from his shocked reaction, I honestly believe he never thought I would call him on his bluff, that I would just stay out of fear of losing everything. He opened the laptop up on the kitchen bench and took everything I had, leaving me with a few dollars in my account. I couldn't believe he was doing this to me, but it didn't change my mind – not one bit. If anything, it made me want to leave even more. Once he slammed the screen down, he simply said, 'Pack your things and go.' I did just that.

What I didn't realise when I'd committed to leaving was that he wouldn't allow me to take my babies with me. It broke my heart when he announced the kids would stay with him. I was already packing and I knew I couldn't back out. *If I do, we will be back to square one.* I didn't know how long it would be until I saw my babies again, but I had faith that I would get it all sorted. Walking out of the door that day was one of the hardest things I've ever had to do, but I also had a steely determination and knew I had the support of close friends who would be by my side until I'd set everything right and had my children with me again.

After David's initial shock and outburst, he knew he couldn't keep the kids and he said, 'Well Janelle, you can have the kids back when your place is set up for them.' Instead of fighting him, I worked hard to get everything ready. It wasn't about revenge on David, it was about breaking free to give myself and my children a better life. It took me eleven days to get my babies back with me and then we had to work out a shared custody arrangement.

David was still trying to play any card of control. He had his own 4WD, but he demanded the Prado as well and I was only allowed it on the days I had the kids. When I didn't have them, I'd have to walk everywhere. I couldn't carry groceries due to my injuries, let alone walk to the supermarket and carry them all the way home again, so I relied on my closest friends to help me out or I'd make sure to do a big shop on the days I had the car.

I was so focused on keeping a positive mindset and listening to my inner voice, trusting that my own guidance and decisions were the right ones. I have always had a strong ability to focus in on what matters most and to pay no attention to what I call the sidelines of resistance of life. My inner voice was telling me, *Janelle you are strong and you know the truth of your situation. It doesn't matter what else is happening, stand with love and be brave – braver than you've ever been.*

I had never second-guessed myself and I wasn't about to start. I knew in my heart this was exactly where I needed to be and exactly what I needed to be doing. By leaving a loveless home and staying true to myself and the promise I made myself all those years ago, I was free to create a new path, have new adventures and to heal not only the physical injuries but take my emotional, mental and spiritual healing to depths that allowed me to face my shadows and release myself from them. Only by making friends with my shadow parts, did I find my strength – even as a child – to free myself from the darkness.

I knew creating some stability for myself and the kids was my number one priority. I needed to work, I needed a car, and I needed both of them quickly. When thinking about this, I dreamed of opening my own salon. My goal was to regain movement in my left hand and fingers so I could be a hairdresser again. I knew I had the skills and the reputation, but it had been nearly two years since the accident.

Hairdressing to me was always like a tool in my life toolbox. I loved how someone could walk in with the weight of the world on their shoulders and, within an appointment, could transcend the negative weighted image of self into the lightness and beauty they want to see and feel. There was my magic. There was my creative outlet. There was my new beginning. It was all the fuel I needed and with a little more work on reactivating my left hand, I opened Meek HD. It was my magic place. A place where I dared to dream and also for my clients to feel they had a place to come and be a part of something magical.

Through my example of staying true to myself and my children, David started to talk to a psychologist and learned how to heal for himself. He learned how to love and how to be the father he wanted to be. That, to me, was the most important thing. All I ever wanted was for my children to grow up with love. We didn't have the perfect home, where we all lived under one roof, but it turned out that being separated and co-parenting was the best we could do; to provide that environment for our children in two homes. David really impressed me at the start of the separation with the amazing work he was doing, but not for one second did I ever think of returning to what was. My children were happy, safe and loved, so my heart was full.

I found my dream car – Jeep Grand Cherokee, gun metal grey in colour with a black grill and black rims – and I bought it. I'd opened the salon and bought the car, all without telling David. It was none of his business anyway. The day I picked up my new car, I was also due to pick the children up. Oh! The joy I had rolling up to the front of his house, lowering the dark tinted windows and beeping the horn. Maddie and Jayden came running out, so excited by what they saw, and David's face was priceless. He stopped still in his driveway and as I got out of my car. I threw the keys to the Prado at him and just laughed as I said, 'Come on kiddies, come see mummy's new car and new hair salon!' With the highest of highs, I placed both my children in their car seats with the help of David's dad. Joseph patted me on my back and said, 'Well done Janelle, I knew you could do it.' With tears in both of our eyes, I drove away singing with the children in the back seat, full of hope and dreams for a new life.

Chapter 12

The Twin Flame

As time went by I had thoughts of starting dating again, one night I was enjoying a few wines with my girlfriends and they encouraged me to join online dating. This was such a foreign thought to me as I'd never done it before. I was so naïve to the dangers and trickery that transpired with the whole process I just trusted and thought everyone on there was honest like me and the concept of chatting to multiple potentials was nerve-racking.

My life changed forever when I saw this man. His sandy blonde hair and sparkling eyes held a depth of mystery that was positively captivating. His name was Liam and he had a strong sense of passion, knowing just how to verbalise himself in a way that made me feel so alive, so attractive, so desirable.

From the outset, he had the power to command my attention. It was six months post my separation from David, and Liam had an alluring energy that held equal parts light and dark. I let my guard down and allowed myself to free fall into a world of passion with Liam. He made me feel like I could do anything and be anything when I was with him. The passion in our life and the way we loved each other was so intense, it was as if it had its own energy force. We could sense each other in such a powerful way. It was unlike anything I had ever experienced before.

Liam was a builder by trade, but wanted to get into project management.

He had a one-year-old daughter named Mia, who I bonded with immediately. She was a very anxious child that was clearly traumatised by something, so I shared a special connection with her. After what I went through as a child, I had a soft spot for children like Mia. I know children aren't naturally naughty or anxious; events and trauma cause that to grow in them as they try to navigate their little lives. It was this understanding that connected me to her. I often wondered what it was that had hurt her and why she was the way she was, but I didn't dwell on it for too long.

Liam would tell me horrific stories about the relationship with Mia's mother, Sarah. He told me how he didn't trust her with Mia and I felt empathy for him and his daughter. I never wanted to fix the situation for him, but I cared so much for him and just wanted to be a part of their lives. Our relationship progressed fairly quickly; we just couldn't get enough of each other. The drama with Sarah seemed to increase the closer Liam and I became. At the time, he lived with his mate Allan in a house in Peregian Beach. It was a party house, which was not very clean nor safe for Mia. We had only been seeing each other for a few months before Liam asked if he could stay at my house whenever he had

Mia, so she wouldn't be in that environment. 'Mia has never been calmer then when she's with you, Nell,' he said. That pulled at my heart strings and I agreed to the idea.

There was one day that stands out in my mind. Liam and I were at his place getting Mia's things ready, as she was about to be dropped off by Sarah. As the time approached for her to arrive, Liam said with such urgency, 'Sarah's crazy and she'll lose it if she sees you here. I need you to go into the spare room and not say a word till I give you the all-clear. Trust me Janelle, it's the best for you and Mia. I'm just protecting you both. You are my girls and I love you.' My protest at being hidden away faded as soon as those three words were out of his mouth.

'Hang on, wait. What? Did you just say you loved me?'

'Yes Nell, I love you. Quick! Sarah's knocking on the door.' I did what I was told and while I was standing in a dusty old room filled with books and bits and pieces, I looked around, not wanting to touch anything. My head and heart were so confused. Here is this strong, confident, sexy man that has the bluest eyes and a lean, but muscular body that was a tower of strength. *How could someone who just said they loved me tell me to hide in this dark dusty room where the only natural light creeps in under the closed door?*

My thoughts were interrupted as I heard Sarah say, 'Liam what's going on? Why are you acting strange?'

'Not today Sarah, I've got plans with Mia.'

Without argument, she left quietly and I could hear Mia running around giggling. Sarah had sounded composed and together and it shocked me, to be honest, because it was the complete opposite to the stories he'd told me. *Who am I to doubt or question him? He is saying and doing all the right things with me!*

Our relationship was bliss. We'd go away for weekends and he would spoil me with beautiful dinners to say thank you for allowing him and Mia to stay at my place. I was moving into a new house within a few weeks and it had so much more room than the little two-bedroom seaside unit I was in.

The first red flag moment happened just before he moved in. He was running a bath for Mia and hadn't checked the temperature of the water. I looked at him and the emotions on his face and the tension in his posture were off. It seemed to me that he was frightened of the feelings he was experiencing, almost like he knew what he was about to do but was internally fighting a war within.

Mia's anxiety was hitting the roof and she wouldn't stop crying. Apparently, she hadn't slept all night and he was very tired.

'WOULD YOU JUST STOP CRYING!' he yelled with a fire that made me jump. When he saw my reaction, he quickly softened and gave me a big cuddle.

'Sorry Nell, I'd never yell at you like that. I've just had no sleep and I hate living here. I can't deal with Mia when she's throwing tantrums like this, it just stresses me out so much. I just need to get her in the bath and then let's just go to your house, okay?'

I agreed and was getting Mia's clothes ready for her as Liam called her into his bathroom. The next minute I hear this high-pitched screaming and I heard the severe thump on the wall. I ran into the bathroom and found Mia on the floor by the side of the tub crying her little eyes out with Liam standing over her in rage.

'It wasn't my fault! I didn't fucking check the water; it was a mistake. I'm just exhausted.'

Instead of seeing the warning signs, I instinctively picked Mia up and carried her to her bedroom to dress her and defuse the situation.

I thought the best thing to do would be to encourage him to just move into my house like he had suggested beforehand, so he would have extra time to look for a place for him and Mia. I would also then be able to help him so he didn't get so stressed with his daughter. Little did I know, I had just witnessed the first sign of the monster that was waiting for me. The monster that would lead me through deep, dark, twisted turns, crippling trauma and soul-destroying moments in the very near future.

It had been so long since I had left my parents behind, I had allowed myself to believe that no one was going to inflict pain or violence on me ever again. I thought I had healed that part of me and that my life was on a trajectory towards happiness. I had allowed a man into my life who loved me and who loved my children and who wanted the best for me.

For six months, we enjoyed camping holidays together and had the most magical time. There were a handful of things Liam said or did that made me uncomfortable, but I chose to turn a blind eye to it because the good far outweighed the bad.

Liam's work was running out and he was stressing over it. He wanted to get into project management and get off the tools altogether. He had charm and a direct way of getting things done, but some people were scared of him and that is why they conformed so readily to his requests. Whenever we were out together, he'd always make sure everyone knew I was with him and that was that. I'd party with his friends and would get comments like, 'What's someone like you doing with Liam?' I'd take it as somewhat of a compliment and laugh it off.

I don't remember there ever being a conversation about him moving in permanently, but sure enough Liam was living with us and he had no intentions of moving. He was there to stay and I couldn't be happier, because he loved me. We would laugh together and we had such a passionate sex life; he just worshipped my body. The playfulness, adventures and pleasures in our relationship counteracted the doubts I had. Liam showed me the playful side of life and I was hooked. I fell stupidly in love, let all my walls down and exposed my deep inner vulnerabilities. This is something that I had never done before, so I had never felt the power of unconditional love that is linked to that level of connection to someone.

The attachment between Mia and I grew stronger and stronger. The sweet little girl would call me 'Mumma' purely because she would see and hear Maddie and Jayden call me that and to her, we were family. For my two, the five of us were family. To Liam, it appeared to be something else. It was like there was an inner conflict because a family is something he told me he wanted, but he also expressed how guilty he felt for loving and enjoying my children and me more than he did his own daughter. He said it was largely due to the stress he'd experienced with Sarah and Mia's constant upsets.

It was only a few months into him living with us that Sarah contacted me saying he had still been staying at her house before he moved into mine; that he had made promises to work things out with her so they could be a family again. I questioned him on this and he told me Sarah had a drug problem and was always smoking weed, so he didn't feel comfortable leaving Mia alone with her and would sleep on her couch sometimes. He showed me photos of her when she was clearly under the influence and who was I to doubt any of what he was saying? If anything, I fell even more in love with him because he was protecting his daughter. Sarah would warn me through texts and emails of Liam being violent and cheating and told me stories of what his family life was like growing up. He always had a plausible and highly detailed story to counteract anything Sarah said, so I ignored her warnings.

I was, however, curious when she mentioned Liam had also suffered abuse when he was younger and I asked why his sister seemed to be scared when she was around him and his parents.

'Come on Nell, you more than anyone should understand that no family is perfect,' he said. I started to believe anything he said to me and showed him love and kindness. He had my complete trust.

Liam sat me down one night and shared his dreams of wanting to earn BIG money. He had these beautiful plans for our future, he was super-supportive of my business and he was so good with my children. He convinced me that doing fly-in fly-out work would be amazing, not only for his career, but for our family and our future. I was besotted with him and felt secure that he was factoring me and the kids into his bright and successful future, so I supported him wholeheartedly.

He'd apply for all sorts of jobs but was unsuccessful due to lack of experience. I had a client at the salon who ran a big commercial construction company that did works all over Australia. I mentioned this to Liam and suggested perhaps I could have a chat to him and see if there was any work in the areas he needed experience in. It was one small way I could show him I was supportive of his dreams for a future. He enthusiastically agreed it would be a great opportunity, so I followed through. The next time Nathan was in the salon, I mentioned it to him and everything fell into place seamlessly. His company was looking for a project manager to run a few smaller builds and if that worked out, it would open more opportunities for Liam.

Liam's anxiety would increase when big changes were on the horizon and when he was stressed. This interview represented a chance for him to get his foot in the door when so many had been closed in his face already, so his stress was peaking big time. I was going to watch Mia at home while he went in, but he begged me to go. 'Nell, please come! I can't do this without you. You are my everything and without you I wouldn't even have this opportunity. I'll have Mia anyway, so afterwards we can all go do something together to hopefully celebrate.'

Wanting to do anything I could to reduce his stress, I drove Liam to the interview and waited in the car with Mia as he went inside. His charm worked once again, and he got the job.

We had a great celebratory dinner at my favourite Japanese restaurant, and I had never seen him so happy, so free, so positive. He kept holding me and thanking me for believing in him, not just listening to what everyone else was saying about him. He said he'd never been loved the way I showed him love, and he would never let anything bad happen to me or any of the children. That night was so pure and so true. The magic was real, our love was real. We laughed together, we danced together, and we made beautiful plans for our future.

Chapter 13

A Hint of Deception

While everything with Liam and I was a complete state of bliss, I had noticed that he and Sarah were struggling to communicate in a positive way and the stress was increasing around their co-parenting. Little Mia was being torn between them both, and I'd spend many nights cuddling her to sleep. She was four by this stage and her anxiety was increasing; her emotional outbursts were reaching a very distressing level.

She'd be playing happily with her dolls and hear her dad raise his voice on a phone call and she'd start shaking and screaming for him to stop. I'd calm her down and reassure her that she was safe and her Nell would always protect her. Liam would not cope well with Mia when she was so emotional. He'd punch walls, slam doors and yell out of frustration because he couldn't settle her. She'd have nightmares and lay crying for me, pushing her dad away when he came to her. I had a clear boundary in place to protect my children; they would not come to stay with me until Mia had settled in again, and she'd ask for her brother and sister. That way, they were protected from Liam's high levels of stress and Mia's outbursts on the first night or two she stayed with me.

The kids all loved each other so much; they played so well. When my children were home with just Liam and I, it was all light and playful; he'd spend so much time playing with them and we all enjoyed ourselves. But when Mia was there, it was different. I watched his heart be torn by the guilt he had for loving my children when he was already a dad to Mia. I'd usually plan some sort of outing that involved us all playing and tiring all the children out; like going to Australia Zoo, indoor play centres, parks, the beach or riding our bikes and having picnics.

Then when we'd get home, I'd do everything and Liam would generally go to the pub with some friends till I had put the children to bed. Then I'd message him, and he'd generally come home. There were times he didn't, but I didn't mind. *He is working hard and blowing off tension with the boys, which isn't such a bad thing,* I thought.

Other times he'd just have a few beers at home depending on how Mia was.

Liam and Sarah went to mediation and worked out a parenting plan that I was included in. Liam was making it clear to Sarah that, in his eyes, I was there to stay.

Everything seemed to be falling into place. That was, until my laptop had gone flat, and I had some emails to send so Liam called out, 'Just use mine Nell, it's on the couch.'

His Facebook Messenger was still open and as I got to work, a message popped up at the bottom corner of the screen.

'Hey you are you free to chat now?' I could see that it was from a woman, but I didn't recognise the name.

My heart raced as I felt sick, shocked and gripped with sadness and anger all at once. The kids were there, so I didn't want to call him out immediately and cause a scene, so I went to the corner of the couch that was against the wall so he couldn't peer over my shoulder, and I'd see him if he came into the room.

Deciding to play detective, I opened the message.... *Oh My God.*

Nothing could have prepared me for what I found. The sex talk was intense. The photos were pornographic. They were making plans to catch up. Judging by the length of the exchange between them, it was clear every time my back was turned, he was contacting her. She seemed to know all about me, but his messages said he was leaving me and planning a trip to Italy with her.

Just then a message from him popped up.... *Wait, what? I'm literally sitting here in the same house as him and he is on his phone while watching the kids play and messaging her.*

As much as I was sick in my stomach, I couldn't look away and as she messaged him back, the sex talk started up.

With tears rolling down my face, I sent my work emails and closed the computer. My children had to be dropped to their dad's, so I got them organised and as I walked past Liam, he saw I was upset. I said nothing to him until I went to leave, calling over my shoulder, 'You really should close your Facebook messages. I saw everything....'

With that, I drove away.

He called me over and over, but I didn't answer. I held myself together for the kids and dropped them off with a big smile on my face, masking every emotion that was running rampant inside me. I had three days before they were due home and Liam was leaving the next day to go out of town for work, so I figured I'd just be silent and think things through before I started asking questions. I had seen how he could lose his temper and I was in complete shock.

I returned home and walked up the stairs and went directly to bed. I didn't want him anywhere near me.

He pleaded with me to listen to him, so I rolled over with tear-stained cheeks and decided to engage. I looked at him and said, 'Why? Who is she?' He saw the pain in my eyes and started crying too. 'She's no one Nell. I've never even met her. She requested me on Facebook and I accepted, then we just started talking and it got out of hand. It's not real! I've never met her in person!'

'Liam, you're planning on taking her to Italy. You've told her so many lies about your life and me and the family. Why would you do that? Please just leave me alone I don't want to be near you right now.'

Realising that he wasn't going to melt me as he had always done in the past, he punched the wall out of frustration and started yelling as he left the house. Where he went? I didn't know and at the time, I didn't care.

He came home early the next morning, grabbed his clothes for the work trip and left in silence. It suited me just fine as I had nothing more to say to him. In his rush to leave, he forgot his laptop and he was away for a couple of weeks, so I thought I'd go through the messages in more detail. More messages came in from her that night and I felt disgusted by what they contained.

I screenshot the messages and sent them to Liam with a short message, 'We are over Liam. What the hell are you doing?'

The next message I saw from this woman was sent to me directly.

'You win, he loves you more than he would ever love me. Enjoy him for me.' Within seconds, my phone rang. It was Liam....

My blood boiled as I answered and I just wanted to scream at him. I started to do just that, but was stunned into silence when I heard him sobbing on the other end of the line.

'I found out it was a fake account Nell. It was actually a dude that gets off on that sort on messaging. I'm so embarrassed and ashamed.' As he was talking, he sent me links to a psychologist he had booked for when he returned home as well as copies of the email he sent to them outlining what was going on. I was still shocked by his emotional cheating, but he was taking accountability for his actions and was going to get help.

I didn't let him straight back into my bed when he came home. We went to a few psychology sessions together when he was home, but because he was temporarily working away at the time, it was more difficult for us to mend things. But we were both committed to trying.

After a few months, he and I started to share our bed again and he was more loving towards me than ever before. I, on the other hand, was guarded and he could feel that. He never pressured me at all, so we took our time and I slowly let my walls down once more.

Then he surprised me with a trip to New Zealand, with no expense spared.

'Tell me gorgeous, what would you like to do in NZ? You name it, and we'll do it. You deserve it. You've stood by me when no one else would have, and I love you so much beautiful.'

As I made us both a coffee, I just smiled and thought to myself, *This can work*. I wanted to believe in him.

We sat and planned such an amazing trip and emailed it to our travel agent to organise everything. We had two weeks to plan care for the children, pets and arrange time off work.

The buzz of excitement just made those two weeks fly by.

The children were all too young to understand where we were going, but they could see how happy we were to be having a couple's holiday.

We dropped our puppy to the dog sitter and headed to the airport with a real sense of adventure and love in the air. We checked into the international departure lounge and ordered a glass of champagne. With bubbles in one hand, Liam lent forward and took my hand with the other and looked into my eyes, 'Nell, I love you. Thank you for being you, thank you for not giving up on us. This holiday is a fresh start and I promise that we will never have to go through that ever again. You deserve so much happiness and together we have that.'

I sat there with tears of happiness, 'Liam I believe in you, and I believe in us. Let's have the best holiday and create memories that will last a lifetime.'

We arrived at the Queenstown International Airport, picked up our car and made our way into town. My breath caught in my throat as we stepped into the lobby of our accommodation; I had never seen anything more beautiful. The place exuded style and elegance with intriguing architecture and wooden floors in such a rich depth of colour with a stone fireplace crackling away, warming the luxurious leather lounges. Alluring works of art gave the room a vibrancy that was only matched by the beautiful, friendly staff.

Upon checking into our King lake-view suite, overlooking Lake Wakatipu with views to the jagged peaks of the Remarkables, we got changed and went to the bar that had even more spectacular views. As we sat together talking and enjoying a beautiful bottle of red wine, it began to snow. *How magical!* I felt so blessed, and completely swept up in the moment.

We spent the next two weeks exploring NZ, trekking the peaks, snowboarding, going on the jet boats and wine tours, driving the coastline. We finished our trip at Fox Glacier and drove to Christchurch the following day to fly home. Our trip was absolutely heavenly!

On our flight home Liam dropped a bombshell; he told me he had decided to apply for a job in Kununurra – an outback town in Western Australia. It was completely random, but I felt as though he'd had it on is mind our whole holiday. I was on such a high and just so happy that I took on the suggestion with a relaxed attitude.

'Nell you can trust me and remember the happiness from this trip. Nothing will ever get in the way of our happiness ever again princess,' he said tenderly.

'Okay, let's talk about this more when we get home,' I replied, still blissed out. I couldn't prepare for what came next. He told me he had already applied for the job and he had an interview the day after we got home.

I felt completely blindsided. *How did this happen?* I felt we were in a really good place, he was going to therapy and he was putting a big effort in at home to work as a team with me, and the children could all sense the love. *Why does he want to work away? And so far away? He just got a parenting agreement sorted out with Sarah*. I just didn't understand. This complete 180 was unexpected and I turned to him with tears in my eyes.

'It's so far away! How long would your roster swings be?'

'Oh my beautiful Nell, don't be upset. It will set us up so well and the job doesn't start till the new year, so we still have four months before I'd have to start. The swing is six weeks on, eight days at home.'

'That's too long, I don't know how we will all cope.'

'Relax Nell, it'll be fine, I promise. I will keep doing the work on myself and always put you and the family first. That's why I'm doing this.'

I sat there on the plane, completely dumbstruck. After filling my heart up with love, adventure, contentment, and all the plans we had just talked about for our future with the hope of being able to move forward and put the past behind us, I was now losing trust in the man I was planning on building that positive future with. *Did he have all of this planned? What am I thinking? Of course he did! He just tricked me. Showered me with love and kindness then pulled the ground out from underneath me....*

The rest of the flight home he held me so tight, just trying to reassure me that everything would work out for the best, but I had a sinking feeling I couldn't shake.

Chapter 14

Torn

Liam aced the interview and got the position. Something changed in him from that moment. He started to miss therapy appointments after he was diagnosed with Borderline Personality Disorder (BPD). I honestly wasn't shocked by the diagnosis, if anything, it was the first time I felt there was hope for him and me. If he got the help he needed, now that we knew what we were working with, he could possibly get better.

He was convinced he was feeling the best he had in ages; he had me and the kids, a nice house and a new job that was such an extreme and sudden decision. This may have made him feel confident and powerful, but I felt more fear and discontent; let's call it an inner knowing that I could sense dark times coming.

He was being so upbeat and happy, it was easy to forget at times he would soon be leaving. We were busy planning a really special Christmas to really celebrate before he started working away for such long periods of time.

It was a Thursday afternoon in November when I picked the kids up from school. I had been feeling a pain in my abdomen all day that was getting more and more intense. Liam was working in Brisbane, so I knew he wouldn't get home for ages. I called David and asked if I could drop the kids to his place as I needed to get to the hospital. I just knew it was bad, really bad. David could hear the stress in my voice and said he would have the children.

Upon arriving at his house I was holding onto the steering wheel so tight, and was hunched over it. I couldn't even sit back in my seat to say goodbye to the kids.

I don't remember the drive to hospital, only a phone call I made to Liam in tears. He left work immediately and rushed as quickly as he could down the Bruce Highway to the Nambour Hospital emergency department, which was more than an hour-and-a-half away.

When he arrived, I was already in a room on a ward with pain meds getting delivered into me via IV, and the doctors were running all sorts of tests. With my history of endometriosis and cysts, they thought I must have had a big cyst burst and were talking surgery.

Liam was by my bedside clearly distressed. He had a very over protective side to him, especially when it came to me. He was getting frustrated with the doctors, and I had to calm him down.

'Liam just let them do their job. I need you to be strong for me. I'm so scared and in so much pain, I just need you to hold me and keep me safe.'

Then the curtains were opened, and a team of doctors

appeared and introduced themselves as members of the oncology and gynaecology unit. They asked if I had a specific specialist I was seeing for my health issues.

'Yes, Kylie Gordon, why?' *Why are they talking to me with such urgency?*

'Janelle, there's a growth on your right ovary. Test results suggest we need to act on this quickly. We will contact Kylie for you and get this happening.' *What does this mean? Do I have cancer? Am I okay?*

I just looked at Liam and lost it, with sadness seizing my body and sending me into a flurry of tears.

'You're leaving me soon for your new job. If it's bad, I don't want to fight this without you by my side!'

He gave me a gentle kiss on my forehead.

'Nell we'll get through this. You're one of the strongest people I've ever met. With everything you've gone through, you've got the fighter instinct and you'll be fine Bub. I promise.'

The doctor's findings pointed to suspected cancer and I was in surgery within three days. I had to sign forms prior to the procedure so that if my surgeon felt it was needed, I would consent to have my ovary removed.

As I woke up in recovery, I asked the theatre nurse, 'Can you please tell me, did they take my ovary?'

With a sadness in her voice, she held my hand and said, 'Yes, darling. Yes they took your ovary. It was for the best and your surgeon will talk to you about it when she is doing her rounds later. Rest now, we will look after you, you'll be taken to your room soon.'

When I woke again I was back in my hospital room and Liam

was sitting there waiting for me. He stayed until visiting hours ended and would be back first thing in the morning to take me home.

I struggled to keep on top of my pain post operation, and it was stressing Liam out to see me in such a state. Each day I got stronger and stronger and two weeks later was the first day I drove again. I was so excited as it coincided with my turn with the children. The happiness I felt to be able to pick them up from school and wrap my arms around them after not seeing them for that amount of time was palpable. I was buzzing as I walked into the school grounds and even the rain that saturated my jacket could not have dampened my excitement. Maddison and Jayden ran up to me giggling and happy, telling me all about their day.

After the kids were in my car, I checked my phone and realised I had a couple of missed calls from Liam and a voice message saying, 'Nell, we need to talk.' I was so swept up in my children that I didn't think anything of it at the time and we carried on with our afternoon.

Liam messaged me later on to let me know he was going out with the boys and wouldn't be home. 'Make sure you and the kids have a great time.' To be honest, it was so nice for it to just be the three of us. I didn't have to share my kids and could enjoy them for the whole night.

◊

A few days passed and I ran into Mark, one of Liam's friends, as I was at a department store buying the three kids new bicycles to hide for Christmas. As we were having a general chit chat, I made a comment about them drinking on a school night. Mark looked at me puzzled.

'When was this? I haven't seen Liam for weeks....'

'Oh… I must be confused,' I quickly responded and made an excuse about the time so I could move on and continue with my shopping.

When I got home, I called out to Liam to help me carry them upstairs and he seemed really angry at me for asking for his help.

'Why are you cranky? You know I'm still recovering. You were meant to come with me to pick them up, but you were late again so I had to go by myself. The least you can do is carry them upstairs please. He huffed and puffed about it, but he went outside to get the bikes and I came into the kitchen to put down my handbag. Liam's phone was on the kitchen bench and as I walked past it, it buzzed. I looked down to see a message come up from someone called Miss Moneypenny.

I opened the message and nothing could prepare me for what I was about to see.

Naked photos of Liam with this woman. As I scrolled up, I found earlier messages from Liam saying, 'Oh my God gorgeous, last night was amazing. We so need to do that again.' In horror, I scrolled through and saw more from Liam, 'Sorry babe, I can't see you tonight my housemate is having an operation and I said I'd drive her home tomorrow from hospital. I am free after 8pm to call as I'll be finished doing all my housekeeping chores by then.'

My heart raced as I felt rage start from my toes and move all the way to the top of my head. The sound of Liam's footsteps coming up the stairs made me instantly feel sick. *Who was this man? Did I really even know him? How could he do this?* I took a screenshot of her number, even though I didn't know what I was going to do with it at the time. I trusted my inner guidance to investigate further before I made Liam aware of what I knew.

Liam quickly placed the bikes in the spare room and closed the door and muttered, 'I can't wait to start my new job. My life here is just too much....' He grabbed his phone off the bench. 'I'm going to sleep in the spare room so you can rest without me bumping you during the night. You need to heal, beautiful. The kids and I need you to be the strongest you can be for all of us. Love you Nell.'

I walked to my room, closed the door and ran a hot shower in the ensuite bathroom. I just sat on the shower floor crying as I grappled with the surreal feeling of knowing the man I love had a secret side that I had just uncovered. The distrust in our relationship was washing all over me. *The signs were there Janelle! Oh, they were there all right! But how am I getting out of this one?*

The next morning Liam had left early for *work*, but I wasn't convinced that was where he was going. I decided to message the phone number. I could hardly be mad at her, she had no idea that he was in a relationship. He was also lying and betraying her trust.

'Hi, you don't know me, but I am Liam's partner. We have been together for a few years and co-parent three beautiful children. We live in Coolum Beach together. It has come to my attention you are sleeping together and starting your own relationship. This breaks my heart and I just want you to know. I'm not upset with you, after all he is lying to you as well, you are just not as involved as I am.' I sent a family photo with the message.

The talking bubble flashed on my phone. *She is responding....*

'Hi Janelle. My name is Candice. OMG I'm so angry! Ahh he seemed so genuine and had a full life story about you as apparently you had been like family for such a long time, and he lived with you to help you out as you had a rough life and had no one else. He said he couldn't catch up on certain days as he was helping you with either your salon or home, which I thought was so kind and a big part of my attraction – finally a man who had good morals. I'm going to go off at him. How could he do this?'

I decided to call her after that, as I dialled her number and was waiting to see if she'd even answer, my mouth was dry as I sat on my front deck gripping to a pillow with a mixture of emotions.

'Hello, Janelle is that you?' A lady's voice answered and I momentarily lost my ability to talk. I took a deep breath.

'Hi, yes sorry it's me. I just called to talk, if you are open to that?'

'I didn't know about you, well, I did, but not in the way you told me. What an asshole! I'm not letting him get away with this and neither should you Janelle.'

Her tone of voice told me she was probably even more mad than I was. 'Candice, Liam is smart and strong. He will have a story all ready to tell us both to make you believe I'm the liar and visa versa. We have to play his game back to him to catch him off guard.'

We organised for Liam to come to my salon, where Candice would be having her hair done. It was a public place and we could play it dumb and not let him think that we both knew what he was doing. We would put him on the spot and see if he felt uncomfortable. On the day, he walked in and took one look at Candice in the chair and said, 'I can see you're busy. I'll head home for lunch and call you.'

Yes it worked! The fear in his eyes was all we needed to see, but we had no idea what would come next. My phone started going off with message after message. 'Nell, that woman you are looking after, you need to know she tried to hit on me the other week and has been stalking me ever since and now she's in your salon. Nell she's crazy. Please get her out of your space, beautiful.'

Then, sure enough, Candice's phone went off in her face, she was just staring at the screen in total disbelief.

'Wow! He's good, I'll give him that. If I didn't meet with you Janelle, I would 100% believe him and what he is saying.'

Her message from Liam said, 'Hey gorgeous, that's my housemate's salon you are in. If she tells you that we are together, don't believe her. She is obsessed with me and that's why I'm trying to find my own place. She'll probably tell you that we've been together for years. I once slept with her and that was a big mistake. Call me when you leave and I'll meet you somewhere. Please don't believe anything Janelle tells you, you're the only one I want to spend time with!'

I just stared at her when she finished reading it out and I burst into tears. I was so angry and hurt. Candice's reaction was one of pure rage, she just wanted to abuse him and tell him where to go. My reaction wasn't as quick as hers as my heart was far more invested and the sting of the betrayal was still smarting. Before I knew it, she had dialled his number and when he answered she wasted no time in telling him exactly what she thought of him. Her take down was nothing short of impressive and her parting words to him were, 'Don't you come anywhere near me again.' She hung up and instantly blocked his number.

'Be safe,' she said while giving me a hug. 'I have a feeling I might have just really pissed him off.'

With my anxiety levels so high, I didn't know what to do. I had to finish my day in the salon and pick the children up. *Is he going to even be at home when I get there? Will he be angry at me? Or will he lie to my face and make up some big story?*

I felt so sick from it all.

I was surprised to find Liam at home when I arrived. He was waiting with my favourite bottle of wine and a beautiful platter of food. He also had a gift for both the children, which I understood was a distraction for them to play with so we could have time alone.

He looked at me with a nervous smile with his arms reached out to me. I knew he was unsure of how I was going to react to him after the events of the morning. 'Nell, I'm sorry. I'm so sorry, I really messed up. I just got carried away in the moment and I took it too far.'

I hadn't even sat down and the children came running out so happy and excited. 'Thank you for our presents Liam! Mum! Look what we got!' He knew just how to play the game and knew how strongly I felt about arguing in front of the children. After what I went through as a child, I promised myself I'd never fight in front of them. That I would conduct myself in a respectful manner and pick my time.

I lowered my sunglasses over my eyes to hide my tears and swallowed the lump in my throat, pushing the emotions down and being the better person in front of my children.

They ran back inside and Liam asked me to sit with him on our outdoor lounge overlooking the beautiful mountains as the sun was setting. At any other moment, it would have been the most romantic setting, but I blankly gazed out to the horizon in wonder of why he would do this to me and to our family.

He tried to hold my hand, but I pulled away. 'We will talk once the children go to bed and tomorrow, when they go to their dad's, I want you to pack your things. Please Liam, you did this, and I don't need to have it in my life.' He grabbed my hand with such force that I couldn't pull away any longer and he looked straight into my eyes.

'Don't do this Nell. I'll go back to the doctor and get more help. I can't lose you... I love you!'

It was always so hard to hold my resolve when he was like this, but I had been hurt so badly that I was not so ready to crack this time.

Once I had put the children to bed, I went straight to my room where Liam was waiting. He had a distressed look on his face. 'Nell, you don't understand. Please let me explain....' He went on to tell me how he met Candice, he even showed me. He was on dating sites. Not just one, but four of them; Tinder, Adult Friend Finder, Redhot Pie and Plenty of Fish. He thought if he shared this with me, I'd somehow understand him and just allow the way he was to continue.

'I have a need Janelle. It has nothing to do with our sex life or our relationship. I just needed to be wanted and played with by women. I get turned on by the risk of you finding out. It didn't start that way, but it quickly grew into a fantasy and it's like I'm addicted.'

'I think this is more than a sex addiction Liam. I think you need more help. Maybe your personality disorder is getting out of hand again since you've stopped going to therapy. I mean, you randomly took a job so far away, and for such long periods of time you won't be home.'

He sat and listened to me, never once interrupting. But once I had finished talking, he picked his phone up and threw it across the room, dinting the wall with its impact. He grabbed me and shook me.

'Why don't you understand? No one else matters to me. They are just easy and fun. I want you and you are mine. You can't just leave me and I'm not packing my things. Mia comes tomorrow and then it's nearly Christmas. I'll go with you to a different psychologist, perhaps one that specialises in sex addictions.' He left the room in a huff and I just laid there crying. I saw the monster that night and he was becoming worse. But all sorts of thoughts were running through my head. I felt a glimmer of hope that I loved him enough for him to feel safe. *Maybe he will get the help he said he wanted.* I wrestled with the light and dark of Liam. There was a struggle between what I felt when times were good and the empathy I had for him going through so much self-inflicted pain, as well as fear of the worst happening to him or to me. It was a constant tug of war between my heart and my mind and here I was, stuck helplessly in the middle.

Chapter 15

Uncertainty Creeps In

We went to see a new psychologist together, and they suggested that as part of the treatment, I should have my own account online with Liam so that I could see what his patterns were and be able to show support. They described it as a desensitisation process, because knowing I was in there too would lessen his excitement and desire for the challenge of catching another woman. I thought it was absolutely crazy talk, but Liam begged me to try. He convinced me it would be for the best, especially with him starting to work away very soon.

I agreed and reluctantly signed up, creating my own profile to be supportive, but it backfired when the requests from others were being directed towards me and not him. He wasn't getting the attention he wanted and it angered him so much. The verbal abuse started to get worse to the point where, as he was yelling, he would froth at his mouth. I was so scared constantly. By Christmas, I had become more aware of some of the things that set him off and realised it was heavily linked to his drinking and drug use. He was indulging in both more regularly, but never when the children were around. He also never gave in to angry outbursts when Maddie and Jayden were around, which I was thankful for. I kept thinking, *It's okay Janelle, hang in there, he's nearly gone. Just play it smart.*

Within the first two weeks of him starting his new job, he called me begging for money. He said he'd spent his wages setting up his new place in Kununurra. I transferred enough for groceries and a little extra, aware he would likely use any surplus at the pub. He would call and message every day and he seemed to be regretting his decision to take the job. Most of the messages said how much he was missing us and he just wanted to come home.

'You wanted this and apparently it was the sacrifice we had to make as a family to get ahead quickly,' I'd remind him. He would agree, but also add that he knew what he was doing, and I had no idea. I was always so excited to see Liam when he came home. Feeling him miss me, and the depth of our conversations while he was away, had grown to make me feel safe and loved. *Maybe he was right. Just maybe, this distance is healthy in some way... for the short term of course.*

There was no action on any of the dating sites he was on and no Facebook messages to other women either. It seemed he was being honest and doing what he promised he would do. When he was home for the eight days, it was all fun time with my kids, time with just Mia and Liam, and we also had our own time, so it was playful and adventurous.

However, Mia started to not cope as well with the absence of her dad. Even when she was with us, she would cry a lot more than normal, and Liam didn't cope well at all with this. I changed the custody with David so they would be home one night with just Liam and I and one night when Mia was there. The kids would be so excited to see each other, they'd run up and down the long hallway with their socks on just so they could slide along the timber floors. But it was unsettling how Liam always seemed to change when Mia was around. The times it was just Maddie, Jayden and me with him, he was so at ease. He would laugh and play with the kids, building Lego with Jayden and singing and dancing with Maddie. It was these sweet moments when I saw a happy future for all of us.

When Mia arrived, it was as though he felt so much guilt for loving my children, he would become anxious. With Mia being a naturally anxious child, she would throw tantrums, break the kids toys and generally act out, which would upset everyone, especially Liam.

The next time Liam left for work, it was almost as though he couldn't get away from us fast enough. His phone was ringing a lot while he was home and he told me it was the boys from the building yards at Kununurra. Their wet season was ending and there was a big race day coming up. When you are isolated like they were, anything events-wise causes a real stir and the whole town gets involved. I was anxious before he left for that stint, knowing the race day was coming up and he held me extra tight that day.

'Don't worry gorgeous, I won't do anything. I know now why I'm doing this, and my head feels good. Mia has just been stressing me out lately, so it'll be good to do something else other than work long days and sit in my accommodation. It will be good to socialize, and not think about you all here having fun while I sit there alone, wondering if I've done the right thing and getting stuck in my head.' I could sympathise with him and understood what he was saying. I just wanted him to be the healthiest version of himself. I was okay with looking after the kids and supporting him emotionally, as long as he did the work to learn his triggers and to gain control of his temper and radical urges.

The day of the races, Liam called me in the morning with the usual chitchat but there were other voices in the background. One woman in particular called out, 'Come on sexy, get your butt in the bus! Come on Liam!'

I asked who that was and he snapped, 'If you don't trust me, fuck off.' And he hung up. I was shell-shocked by how quickly he'd flipped and now more worried than ever he was up to his old tricks.

A few minutes later, I received a text message saying, 'Sorry Nell, I shouldn't of said that. I was just getting on the bus for the races and we've all been drinking. Don't worry, it's all good I love you.'

I had this innate feeling something was wrong, and I asked my friend Lucy to come around for support. A message alert came up on my phone at about 8pm Queensland time, so that was 5pm in Kununurra. It was a photo of Liam with his arm around a female who was dressed up as a naughty sex clown for the races. The message read, 'This is what you get cunt for not trusting me.' I dropped my phone in shock. Lucy picked up my phone and looked at the message. When I saw her shock morph into anger, I burst into tears. She called him, but he didn't answer, so she left a message.

'After everything Janelle has done for you, I can't believe you'd pull this shit. Grow up Liam. You have a family at home and the most forgiving woman I know, if you do something this time you won't be welcome back and I'll make sure of that.'

I looked at her and while it was amazing that she cared so much, I was also so frightened for the backlash from her message. I knew his snap point, but Lucy hadn't seen it.

'Janelle, why are you shaking? What's really going on?' I hadn't even realised that my body had betrayed what was really going on inside my mind and was aghast when I held up my hands and saw they were trembling. Realising the jig was up, I started telling her everything. I hadn't told really anyone because I believed Liam when he'd said people would think I'm full of stories. That I'd look like the crazy one. My silence was exactly what he wanted. He was clever, how he had conditioned me. It was almost as though he had it all planned out from the very beginning.

I felt the most immense relief when Lucy said three little words, 'I believe you.'

'This is really messed up! Oh my God, I want to kill him. What a complete narcissistic prick.' Just as she said that, my phone rang. It was Liam. With everything on the table with Lucy, I put the call on loudspeaker so she could hear.

'Hello….' it was all I could get out before the blasting began.

'What sort of message is that from Lucy? You probably are telling her everything now! She won't believe you. No one will. You're going to look crazy to anyone you tell this to and you know that Janelle, just think before you act. You have a public profile, you have a business and you share custody of your children, you wouldn't want anything to happen to your precious lovely bubble, now would you?' The threats were thinly veiled, and they made my heart sink.

He started laughing and continued, 'I'll do what I want Nell, and there's nothing you can do about it. I'm thousands of kilometres away.' Anger at being spoken to in such a condescending way boiled up inside me. I went to our room and grabbed one of his precious golf clubs, and lined up his surf board against the wall. I needed a release from all of the hurt that was bubbling within, so I started swinging. I smashed hole after hole into his board with the golf club. Lucy didn't try to stop me, she could see the pain I was in. The way she looked at me, it was as if she could feel the pain of my heart breaking.

She just waited till I finished and as I fell to the floor, she just held me in silence.

'I can't do this anymore! I can't let him treat me like this!' I sobbed. Once I'd released all the tears I physically could, I calmed down and took a look at the pockmarked surfboard and the bent golf club.

Oh NO, what did I do? What will Liam do to me when he finds out?

Panic and fear washed over me, but at the same time, a big part of me wanted to take a photo of it and send it to him. *You're smarter than that, get a handle on your emotions.* I decided to give the board to a friend of mine and I just put the golf club back in the bag with the rest of his set.

I didn't get much sleep that night. Liam just kept calling and hanging up, sending abusive messages then apology messages one after another. When I didn't have my children, I always had my phone on just in case David needed me urgently. So instead of turning my phone off and risking missing something important, I was witness to Liam fighting a monster within himself. This frightened me as he was due home in just a few days and I had no idea what would happen, especially when he couldn't find his surfboard. I was terrified.

As Liam's work was getting busier, his mental health was spinning out of control. He had to stay at work instead of coming home for break, so that meant thirteen weeks away. A big part of me was happy about that as I would have time to hopefully plan how I was going to get him out of my house. Sure enough, the remorseful messages and phone calls started. They would be just as intense as the abusive ones.

You see, whenever Liam was taken over by his shadows, the polarity of over giving and being super kind and loving would follow. I would have deliveries of flowers and groceries, the most beautiful letters written to me and spa vouchers sent to my favourite spas. One day I had the blinding realisation, *this reminds me of what I went through as a child with my dad buying me nice things to try and buy my love.* I was becoming more aware of Liam's true nature. The more aware I became, the more I opened my eyes and began to build my own strength and clarity of my own self-worth. He was remorseful and those moments did have the power to suck me back in – I wasn't completely immune to them just yet – so I started to learn how to be smarter than him. I no longer feared him and in some ways I'd had enough.

I thought, *Well Liam's not home for ages now and while he's being sorry for how he has been treating me, I will tell him about the surfboard.*

It had been nearly two weeks since I'd answered any of his calls or text messages. Going off his past patterns, I figured I only had a few days before he would start being very insecure and start harassing me again with aggressive intimidation.

The phone buzzed again and his name flashed up on my screen. *Answer the call!* I psyched myself up and with my heart racing, I took a deep breath and answered.

'Hi Liam.'

'Oh, hello my sweet Nell. I miss you so much! Did you get all the surprises I sent you? I know I lost my shit and you are the last person I want to hurt. You are the only one that really gets me. I just got carried away and was missing you so much.'

'Liam, do you really think that that's enough to make up for what you have done to me and our family? You broke my heart! I've a confession to make. You clearly remember the night with the clown and all the abuse you gave me, right?'

'YES! Nell I wasn't myself. I was so drunk, I don't remember half the night.'

Emboldened by the fact he was thousands of miles away, as he'd so roughly reminded me, I launched into it. 'Well, I took one of your golf clubs and smashed your surfboard....'

He was silent for a while and it terrified me more than receiving another verbal lashing.

'You hurt me so much Liam. I took out all my pain on something you loved. You were choosing other women over me and abusing me. I just lost my cool and I'm not sorry, I just had to be honest with you.'

'Nell I'm surprised you didn't do worse like burn my clothes and change the locks on the doors!'

'I'm not like that.'

'I know, my Nell, you're so much better than that. That's why I hate that I've hurt you so much. I really didn't think it would be this hard to be away from you and the family. I'm hurting Nell. I feel numb to life, like I am losing control.' He choked up as he spoke and started crying.

'Don't cry. You did this, no one else. What am I meant to do from here? I can't change anything. You are just sorry for yourself. I bet if you never got caught cheating, you'd never tell me.'

'I want to see you Nell.'

'NO, you know I can't.'

'Don't leave me Nell. DON'T! I can't do this without you.'

I knew that at this point I had to play along with his game, or I'd be in danger when I saw him next.

'Please, let's just not get into this right now. I'm just about to go to bed, let's chat tomorrow. A video call possibly?'

'Oh baby, yes, you need sleep. I worry so much about you, you are keeping the house, kids and your business together all by yourself. I'm so proud of you. Thank you for talking with me. Night my beautiful Nell, I love you.'

'Good night Liam....' That night I had a sense of relief knowing Liam now knew about his surfboard and wasn't mad... at least for the time being.

My faithful dog Boss was always there for me. Liam and I had got him together in June, 2013, but he was definitely my dog. Boss was a fifty-kilogram English Bullmastiff, but he was my big cuddly bear. I always talked to Boss and he'd lay in bed with me when Liam was away.

Aside from Lucy, I couldn't tell even my closest friends the real truth of what was happening as whenever I started to, their first response would be, 'Just leave him! Why would you stay? Your relationship is toxic, think of the kids, they deserve better too.' There were so many times I'd want to talk to them, but the thought of sitting through another lecture just made me keep my mouth shut. As a result, the darkness and the pain remained locked up inside.

Having Boss with me was a huge comfort, and he always lent me a non-judgemental ear. There is something so deeply spiritual when you have your soulmate as your fur baby. Boss had this look in his eyes like he knew how I was feeling just by sitting next to me. I always said he was the only child of mine I didn't have to share custody of. He was always by my side. When Liam was home and wasn't in the best of moods, Boss would pace up and down where I was almost like he was keeping guard of me. Liam would say, 'That dog looks like he knows I'm off and is worried about you. I swear he is protecting you.' I knew it was true.

◊

I didn't have to go to work the next day, so I went for an early walk on the beach. As I strolled along the sand, feeling the tide wash over the tops of my bare feet in the shallows, I contemplated keeping my word to video call Liam. *I wish I could break free of the pain for Liam and not be controlled by his shadow.* I always had this inner guidance, this power within me, that kept me focused throughout all of my life. Right now, it was telling me *Live Janelle. Be true to yourself. Protect yourself and your children. Go gently.*

I decided that I would honour my promise, and would rather get the call over with. *Maybe when we see each other, it will be enough to snap him out of his pain.* It's a terrible thing when you are so scared of someone that you are frozen in their control over you. I found a place on the beach where I was out of the winds in the warmth of the sun, up on the sand dunes and Boss was with me, which gave me the extra courage I needed. With the time difference, I knew it would be super early and that was another reason why I called; I secretly hoped he wouldn't answer.

After a few rings, I was just about to hang up when he surprised me and answered.

'Oh hello beautiful! Oh how I miss your face. I wish I was with you right now!' In that moment, I felt I was talking to the man I fell in love with at the beginning; the raw, honest, masculine, attentive man that made me feel so safe and allowed me to dream.

I melted into the moment. I cried.

'I wish you never took the job!' We had a beautiful moment of connection and on my walk home, I was thinking of the possibilities of what could've been if he hadn't started the job in Kununurra. My mind was once again playing tricks on me. It was like knowing something is bad for you, but you want it anyway. Deep down, I knew I wasn't happy and it was all becoming so tiring, but I just couldn't bring myself to end it. I felt so beaten, so lost. He had me just where he wanted me.

Chapter 16

The Rescue Mission

We continued to talk every now and then, although I didn't make time for the contact we would normally have. This was one way I was trying to empower myself. We seemed to be tracking along nicely when all of a sudden, Liam didn't seem like himself.

My blood ran cold when I received a text message from him out of the blue that said, 'Nell I'm done. I'm not worth it. I can't live with this pain inside me.' I didn't know how to respond, so I reached out to his mum and dad.

'Tom it's Janelle, ummm, I'm not sure how to tell you this, but I need help with Liam.'

'Hang on Janelle, let me put Beth on as well.'

There was a bit of shuffling on the other end of the line before a female voice said, 'Hello? What's wrong?' Beth had a direct urgency to her voice. I was shaking and unsure of how to break this news to them, but I figured it was best to just come out with it.

'It's Liam. He's been threatening to kill himself. He said he can't live with what he's done to me and the family.'

'Janelle, what do you mean? What has he done?'

I went on to tell them everything and Tom surprised me when he said, 'Get away as quickly as you can, love.'

'Tom! Don't be like that! He's our son!' Beth chided him. 'I'm sure he didn't mean it, Janelle. Sometimes people do things in a moment they don't mean.' There was something in the way she said that which stood out to me. It was like she knew more than she was letting on.

A few hours later, Tom called me back. 'Janelle, I need you to call Cate, but before you do, you need to know something.'

Cate is Liam's sister, and I was totally confused.

'Isn't there a big issue between them? Liam told me Cate's always causing trouble and has deep-seeded mental issues. I wouldn't feel comfortable calling her, can you just tell me Tom? Please?'

'Liam's done this many times before. Once, the police were called because he attacked his sister and another time because he tried to kill himself by hanging himself by his surfboard leash.'

This was all too much! What do they want me to do with this information? Does Beth know Tom is telling me all of this?

'What do you want me to do Tom?' I knew he could hear the pain in my voice because he lowered his voice.

'I know my son, and I have never seen him with anyone like he is with you. It's like he allows his pain to be seen by you instead of running from it. I'm not saying what he has done is right, but love, just maybe you are the one to make a positive change in his life. We all love you and we want to help.'

'How am I meant to do that?' I asked, utterly defeated by the idea that I would have to be the one to save Liam. 'Leave it with me. I'll talk to Beth and call you back.' That night, Liam's calls were so distressing that I even contacted the guys he worked with asking if they could check on him for me. I did it out of love and for peace of mind, but I then got the aggressive Liam calling me.

'What the fuck is wrong with you Janelle? Why would you message the boys? Now you've just made things even harder for me, thanks... just let me die or I'm going to bring you down with me bitch.' The radical pendulum of emotions inside me was pushing me to breaking point. I felt completely lost and alone, unsure of what the right thing to do was.

Then Beth called with a plan.

'Janelle I'll tell you what we need you to do. We need you to get to Kununurra, spend some time with him and hopefully convince him to come home. I just spoke to him. He pretended he was fine and said he was out with the boys having a few drinks. When I asked how you and the kids were, he told me you are all great and how much he misses you all. As his mother, I know what he is doing. Get there.' I protested that I didn't just have the ability to leave home, the kids and work in an instant. But she insisted this was life or death for Liam.

How am I going to organise this? I flew into action with my girlfriends, David and staff at the salon to allow me to have five days off. But before I officially locked anything in, I waited to hear from Liam the following day. He would usually rebound from a snap with a sense of calmness and coherence. I knew he was in a better place the moment I heard his voice.

'Hey Nell! How are you? I miss you. Sorry about the episode the other day I just wasn't myself. I feel better now, just missing home and you.'

This was my opportunity.

'Liam since you can't make it home for a while, how do you feel about me coming to stay with you for a few days? I've organised things here to allow it, I just didn't know if you wanted me to?'

'Are you serious Nell? Yes baby! Yes, please come that would be just what I need. When will you be here?'

'In three days, if you are sure?'

'Oh I love you Nell, thank you for being so good to me. I'll organise some fun things for us to do. I'll have to work two days you're here, but I can come home each day to you and go to sleep holding you.'

I got off the call feeling more confused than ever. I called Tom and said that Liam was very excited for me to go, but I didn't think it was fair that I had to leave my children and my business to help their son. I felt they were putting a lot of pressure on me.

'Send me your account details, we want to pay for your flights,' he said.

It wasn't quite the response that I was expecting, but it was appreciated nonetheless. The next thing I knew, I was on a plane to see Liam. I still wasn't sure exactly what would happen, but I went with an open mind and a guarded heart. The night before I got there, I had a hard time getting hold of Liam. He said he went to bed early as he was excited to see me. I gave him the benefit of the doubt, but when he picked me up, I could smell the alcohol on his breath. He seemed so excited to see me, so I didn't say anything.

We had to stop at the supermarket to grab a few things and when we got to the checkout, I noticed a woman staring at us the whole time, like she was trying to work out who I was and what I was doing with Liam. He picked up on it too and quickly ushered me out to the car.

'Don't worry about the female staring at you, you are new to town and in small outback communities like this, you stand out. They are only just getting used to seeing me around. Forget about it, let's drop this stuff at my place and we'll head to the yards so you can meet the team. That way when you're at home, you know who I'm with.'

I tried my best to brush the awkward glances of the woman off, but I was unsettled and my mind began to race.

'Okay Liam, that sounds good.'

When we got to his unit, I stood in the doorway in complete shock. It was trashed, like he hadn't been home from the night before. He saw me looking around and jumped in with an excuse.

'Sorry about the mess. The boys came over yesterday afternoon and had a few drinks before they went out. I was so tired I just went to bed and got up early for work so I could finish early to pick you up.'

'Oh, I see. So that's why you didn't answer my calls?'

'Nell, it's not what you think,' he said as he rushed to my side and grabbed my hands. 'I love you. It's so nice to see you. Come on, let's go see the boys.'

Driving through the red dirt on the way reminded me of my childhood in Mt Isa, and by the time we reached the yards, the guys were just finishing for the day. The gates were so high and topped with barbed wire, it felt ominous driving through them. We got out and Liam put his hand around my waist holding me as we walked towards the group of men all opening beers to quench their thirst at the end of the day.

'Hey Liam, want one? Or are you still charging from last night you dirty dog!' One of them called out jovially. I looked at him he dismissed the comment with a wave of his hand and a smirk, before turning back to the group.

'Hey boys this is Janelle, my partner. She's just flown in from home to spend a few days with me.' Their mouths all dropped in unison as they looked at me and one by one, they regained their composure and stepped forward to politely introduce themselves. I realised my phone battery was getting low and I wanted to make sure I was contactable in case something happened back home with the kids, so I excused myself to go to the car to put my phone on charge. As I walked away, they thought I could hear them and they started up a conversation. I slowed down my pace so I could take it all in, hoping to understand everyone's weird reaction to me.

'Shut up! Don't say a word. She won't be here for long,' Liam said to hush them. *Um, what was that I just heard?*

Then another guy piped up, 'This isn't right Liam. What are you doing buddy? Why would you jeopardise a relationship with Janelle? Look at her! You need your head read.' No longer concerned about my phone, I turned back around and started walking towards them. I had barely made it back when Liam wrapped his arm around my shoulder and said, 'Come on beautiful. That's enough of these clowns. I can see them another day.'

As we turned around, someone yelled out, 'Ask him about the English guy at the pub last night and why he has a scratch down the side of his face!'

With his arm still holding me close, I could feel Liam's whole body tense up and I knew he was hiding something, *But what?* I knew if I asked him, he wouldn't be honest. *Time would tell.* I was there to suss out his lifestyle and where his head was at, so I didn't bring it up at all on the drive home. Liam went for a shower when we got back as he had made a dinner reservation at the Pump House. It was this amazing restaurant within an old pump house on the river where crocodiles swam and were very active. I was excited to go check it out and just try and forget what I just heard from the boys, but I just couldn't shake it off. I had to ask.

'Liam what really happened last night? Why did you lie to me?'

'I didn't want to upset you. I didn't plan on having a big night, it just happened and I got carried away. There were these backpackers at the bar harassing one of the local girls I could see she was uncomfortable, so I told them to back off but one of them took a swing at me and we ended up in a full-on punch up.'

'So wait, let me get this straight. You first lie to me, then you go out getting blind drunk standing up for some girl at the pub and getting into a fight over her. Did I miss anything? Oh my God Liam, you really are worse than I thought. And now you want me to go to dinner with you? No thanks, I just lost my appetite.'

I sat on the lounge after moving a pile of Liam's work clothes out of the way and couldn't hold back my tears. I saw the photo album of our family next to me on the coffee table and I picked it up.

'Look! Look Liam! This is what you are ruining by doing what you are doing. You call me saying you are going to kill yourself and then you go out 'til who knows what time the night before I arrive to see you. To travel all this way, leaving the kids to try and work out what is going on.'

He kneeled on the floor in front of me with his head on my lap crying.

'Please Nell forgive me. I want to make things right; I'll be coming home the day after you leave here, I requested some personal leave. Let's just go to dinner I really want to spoil you.'

'Liam you just don't understand,' I said as I stood up. 'I don't really want to be near you.' Just as I went to move into another room for some space, there was a knock at our door.

Our lift to the restaurant had arrived; it was one of his mates from work and his wife. *Great! Now I feel ambushed!*

They were going nearby, to the Pump House, so Liam had organised for them to take us so we didn't have to drive. Sometimes it was easier to sacrifice my own happiness to save an argument, plus I had Beth on my mind and her desperation to bring Liam home, so I was feeling pressured from all angles. Despite all of this, I still had this strange feeling, as though all my cells were screaming at me *Run! Get on a plane and go home!* I silenced that inner voice as I stepped into the open car door. The Pump House was nice, but again the looks Liam and I were receiving were making me uncomfortable.

'Do you know those ladies at that table? One of them is the same one that was at the supermarket.'

We had finished our meal and Liam lent over the table and kissed me and then looked straight at the woman I was talking about and said, 'Well, let them look. These people aren't my forever person, you are.'

We paid our bill and went back to his place. I was in no mood for arguing as I was so mentally exhausted, so I went to bed.

The next morning Liam had to go off to work, so I borrowed a Ute from the yards to go off exploring. The town was an odd blend of beauty and darkness and with a diamond mine being the main source of trade and work for the town, there was a real mix of FIFO and residents. I found a sign for Jump Rock, where apparently you could launch yourself from the top into such pure and clear waters. I was keen to do that, so I messaged Liam and he agreed he would take me there once he finished work. He told me he'd borrow a boat from one of the boys to get access to it.

Being out on the water with him was so much fun that for a moment, I forgot all that was wrong with our relationship and just loved the experience. We both laughed and joked around and as I looked at him in the moment. I said, 'Liam this is the best version of you. I love these times, I just can't be with the dark side of you and there seems to be more and more of the darkness than the light these days. You scare me sometimes.'

He gently placed his arm around me and said, 'I hate myself for doing what I've done. I have really messed up. I've always had a temper but I don't know why it comes out directed at you, you are the one I love the most. Maybe it's because I feel safest when I'm with you, I feel I can let it all out as I know how strong you are.'

'So wait, Liam are you saying you feel my love for you is stronger than the pain you cause and therefore you lash out, thinking I'll just always be here?'

'Well where are you going to go? No one will believe you when you tell them. Don't you see? I have you. You are mine.'

The magic that had been in the air dissipated the moment those words left his lips.

'Take me back please, I have had enough.'

As we were on our way back, I just looked out the window reflecting on his words. *He never owned me and I'm not his to own either*, I fumed. I didn't say much that night either, I just went to bed. I decided that I would travel home a day earlier, so that meant I only had one full day left. Liam wasn't meant to work the following day but he had been called in for a few hours, so I went into town to get a coffee and something to eat while he was gone.

I found this cute little café that reminded me of one I went to back home on the sunny coast. It was well furnished and the fit out was playful, the music was very chilled café lounge style and it had super healthy food options. I got chatting to the girls that worked there and they asked the usual questions; where I was from, what was I doing in town, did I know anyone? When I said I was in town to visit my partner as he was missing home and I was worried about him, they asked what his name was.

'Liam James…. Why do you know him?'

The girls looked at each other with raised eyebrows.

'There is someone you need to talk to… her name is Erin. She's a teacher here in town and one of our girlfriends,' one of the women said. When I asked why, they didn't offer any more information, but one of them started texting on her phone.

As I was finishing my coffee, a lady with long brown hair and very neat looking clothing with pale skin walked up to me with an unmistakable sense of purpose. 'Janelle is it?'

'Yes that's right, how do you know my name?'

She sat across from me and told me she was Erin and her friends had contacted her to let her know I was there. She explained for the last few months she had been in what she thought was a relationship with Liam. She knew all about Mia, Maddie and Jayden... even me. Liam had told her my salon was sending us broke and the stress of it all pulled us apart and for him to get back on his feet and provide for the kids, he took the job away. Apparently, Liam and I were no longer in contact.

Erin showed me photos of messages that he had sent her that same morning. My heart broke for her as much as it broke for me. *She seems so nice and has a lot going for her.* I then paused and thought, *If I get up and walk out without telling her the truth, he wins. He still holds all the power.* She reminded me of how I was when I first started dating Liam - love drunk on his playfulness and feeling sad for him and what he had been through. I decided to tell her the truth and called Beth so I had the support to back myself on the things I was saying. Erin was so upset I didn't really know if she believed me as Liam was so good at making us women fall so hard for him that we would doubt anything negative people would say about him.

I thanked her for coming to tell me, and I left her and her friends my number.

'Be careful,' I said softly as I got up to leave. 'He can be very dangerous, so sticking together is the only way to get out of this.'

I had reawakened the warrior within me once again, protecting others and standing up for what I believed in. I felt this ball of fire growing within me. I was ready; I'd had enough. *It is my time.*

I sent Liam a message, but had no idea Erin had called him, telling him everything and saying she never wanted to see him again. I knew that wouldn't be the case. He was such a smooth talker and their relationship was new, so he could still convince her I was the crazy person. He would probably say things to her like, 'Don't worry, Janelle is leaving tomorrow. We just need to sort out a few things regarding the kids and then you and me can move on with our life together.' I knew this innately; he did the same thing to me at the start.

As soon as he got my message, Liam called me back.

'Don't believe Erin, Nell. She has been trying to be with me since I got into town. Apparently there aren't many good male options in town, she would tell me. She's a school teacher where we are building, so we chat. That's it. Occasionally when we're all at the pub, she would join us, but as a group, not as a couple. Believe me Nell.'

I completely lost my patience and was sick and tired of hearing the same old excuses on repeat. *No more.*

I yelled without a care of anyone around me and what they would think of my sudden outburst, 'LISTEN TO ME LIAM! YOU ARE SICK. YOU NEED PROFESSIONAL HELP. I DON'T WANT ANYTHING MORE TO WITH YOU. I'M DONE!'

Chapter 17

Tethered

A few hours and about a 100 missed calls and messages later, he came back to the unit. I had packed my things as I was leaving early the next morning. That way, at least I had a few days to get sorted before he was back for his break. I was sitting in the spare room on one of the single beds when he barged through the door. I took one look at him and instantly slammed the door to the room in his face. He had an emptiness in his eyes, his top lip was turned up in a snarl and the vein on his forehead was popping out so much that I could see his pulse pumping.

I had to use all my strength to hold the door closed to lock it as he had snapped and his strength intensified. He started punching and kicking the door. In horror, I realised the doorframe was starting to break. I took one deep, giant breath and channelled all the pain, lies, and darkness I felt from him and opened the door. I literally had to punch my way out of there. Blow after blow connected to his jaw; I remember just wanting to cause him pain to potentially set him free from this rage. I was so scared, but more than fear, I wanted to be safe again. He dropped to the ground, so I quickly grabbed my bags and ran out past him.

'Look what you have done Nell! Where do you think you're going? Get back here you stupid bitch!' He yelled after me, but his words weren't coming out properly.

I jumped in the Ute because the keys were usually always left in it. But this time, they weren't. I didn't want to go back in there, I doubted my ability to put up another physical fight in order to get to the keys. Plus, I had no idea where they would be. I saw him running towards me, so I locked the doors. When he reached the vehicle, he slammed his hands on the bonnet and laughed in the most maniacal way. It was then that I noticed his jaw was out of place.

'Look what you did to me! I have to fly home to my daughter and will be all black and blue. I'll tell everyone what you did and how you lost your mind. You will lose everything and everyone, I'll make sure of it.'

He shook the car keys in front of me. 'You're not going anywhere….'

I instantly felt the adrenaline leave my body and panic firmly set in. All I wanted was to be home with my children. *What am I meant to do now?* Stuck in the car, I realised I had been so focused on getting away from him, I didn't even realise the injuries that I had sustained in the scuffle for me to get out of the house. I felt him hit me, but it was like I had the ability to shut out the impact at the time. I realised I had visible grab marks and swelling on my shoulders and pain shooting down my ribs.

Liam had walked away from the car, but I knew he would be watching me like a hawk. I lay in the Ute crying for what seemed like hours and hours. I knew Liam would snap back out of this head space eventually, but just how long would that take?

I called his dad and told Tom what happened. He sounded so upset and said he wished they'd never pressured me to go. He said he and Beth would fly from Melbourne to the Sunshine Coast to be there while Liam was back to help me stay safe. I agreed that sounded like the smartest plan.

Time was suspended for me, so I have no idea how long I was in the Ute. But the next time I saw Liam, he approached the car crying and talking in a quiet tone.

'Nell… Nell I'm sorry I scared you. I'm sorry I hurt you. I wasn't thinking clearly. I just got exposed for the truth of who I am and I don't like that. I shouldn't of done any of it. I shouldn't of taken the job here either, please come inside. I'll stay away from you and I'll drop you at the airport in the morning. Please Nell, it's getting dark. Come inside, I'll leave the door unlocked for you.' I didn't move a muscle, so he stood there blinking in silence for a few minutes, before turning on his heel and going inside the house.

I waited in the Ute a while longer. I knew from experience that after he lost it, he would go into a very deep sleep. Once I felt enough time had passed, I very quietly snuck inside. I saw he was asleep on the couch in the lounge room, so I grabbed the keys to the Ute and went into the bedroom. I laid down, but I didn't give in to sleep. I knew I needed to be on alert.

We didn't say one word to each other the next morning and it was a huge relief when he drove away after dropping me off at the airport. *Now what am I to do?* I knew now that I had to get him out of my life. It was almost like I was an addiction for him. He couldn't let me go, he didn't want to, but it wasn't his choice to make.

When he came home a few days later, his parents also arrived as promised. They booked accommodation nearby and encouraged Liam to stay with them and I was surprised when he agreed. I didn't have to see him, except for the last afternoon before he flew out. Mia wasn't coping very well with staying at the hotel with her dad and grandparents. She was missing me and Beth called.

'Love, Mia needs you. Liam is struggling and we are about to fly home, we're on our way to the airport. Can we drop Mia to you please? Sarah is picking her up in a few hours.'

I agreed because I loved Mia like she was my own and I wanted to keep her safe. When she saw me she came running and jumped up into my arms, 'My Nell! My Nell!' *Sweet, innocent girl.* 'Would you like to come play playdough with me? Wave bye-bye to grandma and poppy.'

With that, we went upstairs. I knew this meant Liam would be there soon as the airport was only fifteen minutes away, but I hoped he'd be respectful around his daughter. When he got back, we were watching a movie cuddled up on the lounge.

'Hello, my beautiful girls! Can I sit with you?'

'NO!' Mia said, 'My Nell and me are watching a movie.'

She snuggled in so close to me, I wondered what really had happened while they stayed with his parents. Liam went to the freezer and took out her favourite ice cream - a chocolate paddle pop - and sat down at the other end of the lounge. He held it up and waved it around, almost as though he was bribing her. She wanted the ice cream but didn't want to leave my side.

'Mia loves you more then she loves me! I do really love you Nell, I wouldn't even get to see my daughter if it wasn't for you.'

'Well Liam, you should've thought about that before you did what you did then, huh?'

As much as I wanted to stay where I was, I was busting to go to the toilet and couldn't wait any longer. I got up and Mia went to her dad to eat the ice cream. As I was coming out of the bathroom, I heard her scream. My pulse quickened as I ran to the lounge and I saw Liam pinning her down.

He began yelling, 'IT'S ALL YOUR FAULT! MY LIFE IS FUCKED BECAUSE YOU WERE BORN!'

'STOP! Get your hands off her! Don't you ever do that again....' I braced myself for becoming the focus of his anger, but instead, he picked up his things and walked out in complete silence, leaving me alone with Mia.

I calmed her down and just held her. Sarah arrived shortly after and she wasn't surprised when I told her what had happened.

'Why do you think I agreed to Liam seeing Mia at all? It was because I knew you'd keep her safe. She loves you and you are so good to my daughter. I thought and hoped that just maybe he would change. Thank you for telling me Janelle.'

We sat talking for ages and it turns out that a lot of what was said and done to me was very similar to what happened with Sarah, but she said when they were together there was a lot of marijuana use as well.

Sarah said she had never seen him as happy as he was when he was with me and I had her full support no matter what I decided to do going forward. Sarah asked if I would like to keep having Mia stay with me and the kids as we had been doing. She felt it would be good for Mia as well and to be honest, I wanted to. *Perhaps we could try for a bit and see how it goes?* We planned for Liam to stay at my place, but sleep in a different room while Mia was over. The condition was he had to start therapy again and look for work closer to home.

Sarah had new parenting orders written up and Liam agreed to them. I was terrified; I didn't eat for a few days before Mia's next visit. I had panic attacks and felt so alert the whole time Liam was there, but I had to hide my terror and be brave. I felt a duty of care for Mia, so I just wanted her to know she was safe.

Liam was still working in Kununurra, but he had stopped seeing Erin. She sent me a long message saying that when Liam got back from his home break, he had called her and said they could no longer see each other. But they had still slept with each other a few more times. This still hurt me, as I didn't really know where we stood. I was co-parenting his daughter with his ex and he was still staying at my house when he was back when we had Mia. It was all a big mess, but at least we weren't fighting.

A few weeks later, Erin messaged me in the middle of the night and left a few voice messages as well. Liam was at the pub with a girl. *Wow big surprise; he thinks he's been a good boy for long enough that everyone would've magically forgotten what he had done.* She sent me some photos and I even had a call from the police in Kununurra asking me questions about Liam, which sent my anxiety into a spin. *Why do I care? Why am I worried about him?* I felt so manipulated emotionally and mentally by him that my kind heart was so stressed. I gave the apartment night manager a call and he said at first sign of daylight, he would go to his door to check on him. I was worried he may have just followed through with the suicidal threats, so I informed him of that also. He said he would take the police with him.

I didn't get any sleep that night. I tried over and over again to call Liam but nothing. Not a thing. In the early hours of the morning, I got the call from the apartment manager. They had let themselves into Liam's room and found him in bed with a woman. Her name was Nikki.

She got in contact with me and told me the police gave her my details; I never got an answer as to why they would have done this, so she could very well have been feeding me lies. She told me that during the night she and her family were all at the pub, as she was in town visiting them. She and Liam had started chatting at the bar, and despite her brother warning her not to go home with him, because he'd heard what sort of a guy he is, she had been wooed by Liam's charm and ignored the advice. *Boy he had that game so well played by now, he could write a book on the ways to allure a woman to fall for you.*

I realised he seemed to always go for the confident, successful, beautiful women.

That latest incident signalled the end for his time in that town. It didn't matter how good he was at his job, his personal baggage had made him a liability for the company. They set about transferring him to a new job in Darwin, but first he had a month off to get things sorted, which scared me. I contacted Sarah and we planned to sit down together with him when he got back to talk a few things out. We knew he would come back full of shame, guilt and remorse; it was a pattern we were both familiar with.

We were right, he was in a very low head space. I didn't even feel scared of him when I saw him, all I felt was that familiar sadness. He looked completely broken and asked if he could stay with me and the kids.

'You are the only good things in my life,' he pleaded.

'I'll think about it,' I said. There was a huge part of me that didn't want him anywhere near me, and then there was this part that longed for him to get well. *Maybe, just maybe, what everyone else saw could be right. Just maybe he could get well, and we could be happy.* The moment that voice piped up in my head, the logical part of my mind, which was becoming stronger, would counteract, *What are you doing considering getting back into bed with a monster? Will you ever really be safe?*

But having him home and getting fit and healthy was so nice, I let the dream of being a happy family unit be entertained again. Darwin wasn't as far as Kununurra and his stints away were only two weeks. *Okay, maybe this can work. But is he mentally well enough to handle it?* When I voiced my concerns, Liam convinced me that he was, so I decided we could give it another try.

Chapter 18

The Point of No Return

Three months had passed and everything seemed to be going fine. Liam was not drinking as much and was living in a better environment. The work wasn't as stressful and at least this time the company was also aware of his drinking problem, affairs and violent temper. He had all the support he needed around him. But a work dinner to celebrate the year and the success of the jobs saw everything come unstuck. Liam called me saying he'd had an argument with one of the bosses that were there - it was the same guy that had yelled out the comment about what Liam had been up to when I was in Kununurra.

He had been promoted over Liam and, with a belly full of alcohol, the guy had made another comment about how he couldn't understand how a beautiful woman like me would see anything in a piece of shit like Liam. This set Liam off, firstly because I was mentioned and secondly, because he was called a piece of shit in front of everyone.

Liam sent me a selfie of him sitting outside in the gutter with a caption saying, I love you. I'm sorry'. I didn't hear from him again until later the next day. I could hear in his voice he wasn't right and his mental head space had slipped again. He had two more weeks there until his next break. He had been applying for jobs back in Queensland and received news a big company back home was offering him an interview. They were based in Brisbane but had an office on the Sunshine Coast.

This was good news as it could be the positive change he needed.

He sent me an email from his current employer that read:

> *Hi Liam,*
>
> *Mate, it was clear to me last night that you have some serious underlying issues with working for the company and what it means to you and your family.*
>
> *All we want to do is provide an opportunity. We do believe we provide not only stability but also new experiences and value to be added to people's futures.*
>
> *I would not want to think people are that unhappy working for us.*
>
> *Liam, I think you are an asset to the Company and have always supported you and your work. But if you need a break from us I need to know ASAP.*
>
> *Please consider your future plans and let me know how you want to proceed.*

Kind Regards
Jacob
Construction Manager

Clearly there was more to the story than what he told me, but I wasn't surprised by that either. He needed to find what it was that he was happy with. It seemed to me that the guilt, shame and self-sabotage was just like a drug addict's need for the hit, that adrenaline surge, that fight. He was so stressed he clearly just needed to ground himself, but I feared he was too lost within the shadows that haunted him to ever fully come back to me.

He had the phone interview before he left Darwin and they short listed him. Armed with the glimmer of hope and potential of coming home, Liam handed in his resignation and flew home. But what should've been a happy homecoming was anything but.

I had become very untrusting of Liam and after reading his email from his employer, I started doing some digging before he got back. I opened his phone bill and went through the numbers for the two days that he was unaccounted for in Darwin. After the work dinner he made repeated calls to a local Darwin number so I Googled it, as I was reading the search results, I felt violently sick. It was to a prostitute! *Oh my God! Oh my God! What has he done now? Did he use protection? Did he hurt her? Why would he do that? What do I do now?*

My head was spinning as I paced up and down the length of the house trying to make sense of it all. *Hang on, why am I trying to make sense of him and his mindset?* I realised I could never understand the way his mind worked, I had too much logic to even really know where to start. Even though

I could see his triggers now and felt the shift within him from light to dark, I was also terrified of him and didn't know how to get out.

Unsure of what I would even say, I called the prostitute. She was very closed off and defensive towards me at first. But when I asked, 'Did he hurt you?' She went from being very blunt with me to opening up just a little.

'Look sweetheart, I had to get him removed from the room; he did act out of line and he kept calling me afterwards saying he didn't get enough for what he paid for. I can't go into it anymore for confidentiality reasons. Have a good day. Stay safe. Bye.'

As if on cue, the moment she ended the call, I looked up to the sound of a car door closing and moments later, Liam was standing at the top of the stairs.

As the rage boiled in me, I couldn't even stand the sight of him.

'You slept with a PROSITIUTE?! WHY?!'

He looked super calm as he stepped towards me, but I pushed him away as he reached out for me.

'DON'T TOUCH ME! YOU'LL NEVER TOUCH ME AGAIN!' I called for Boss and got in my car. I just had to leave, even though I had no idea of where I was going. I ended up at the beach and I felt so alone. If I called my girlfriends, they would only give me a lecture and say, 'Janelle, we told you long ago to leave him – but you didn't.' *They wouldn't understand. How could they? Even I don't understand why I stay!* I was trapped, and I was fighting to get out; but it's so much scarier and harder than just packing up and leaving.

My phone kept ringing and the missed calls built up to 40 before I could bear to answer.

'What Liam? What could you possibly say that would change my mind this time?' I could tell he sensed I was done for good this time, and that frightened him.

'Nell I just quit my job and have come back home to make things right. I don't want to be that man anymore. I want help. I *need* help. I know it's not up to you to help me, I just need the week to sort out my things. I'll leave Nell, as I'm the one that messed it all up!'

That afternoon Mia was getting dropped over, and I was getting my children back the next day. *Just get through the weekend without the children seeing any of the drama*, I coached myself. I left home early the next morning to pick Maddie and Jayden up. Mia came with me as she was so excited to see the kids.

It was a really hot day, and I was lying in bed with Maddison as she was still recovering after having her tonsils and adenoids removed and understandably didn't feel up to jumping on the trampoline with the other two. We could see them clearly from her bedroom window. Liam was hosing Jayden and Mia to cool them down as they were bouncing. They were having a great time laughing and playing.

Mia suddenly slipped and hit her head on the safety net pole and bit her lip from the impact. It started to bleed and she screamed at the top of her lungs. Liam grabbed her by her shirt and pulled her off the trampoline in a very aggressive manner. Instead of soothing her, he started yelling and swearing at Jayden, blaming him when he wasn't anywhere near her at the time. I ran outside to defend Jayden, but he had run to the back stairs and was sitting on the bottom step shaking and crying.

'Pull your head in Liam! Jayden didn't touch Mia,' hearing my voice, Mia squirmed her way out of Liam's arms and ran to Jayden and held onto him tightly. I saw Liam pick up a shovel that was lying nearby and it took me a split second to realise he was intending to use it. That look in his eyes... he had snapped. *I have all the kids, how am I going to get us all out of here?* I didn't have any time to register what was happening before my son screamed, and an ear-piercing BANG! erupted nearby. The shovel had missed Jayden's head by mere centimetres after Liam had lobbed it at us like a spear. It was stuck it the cladding of the house, still quivery from the force it was thrown with.

I quickly picked Jayden up by his arms. 'Run Jayden! Run to your sister's room and lock the door, close the window and only come out when I say.'

I didn't have to tell him twice. He was off like a rocket. I turned to get Mia, but Liam was already dragging her away by her feet. As her belly slid along the ground, she screamed for me and tried desperately to claw at the ground and wriggle free. 'Nell...! Nell...!'

Knowing I couldn't take him on without endangering Mia, I went inside to grab my phone and keys and headed towards Maddie's room, but I heard him running towards the back door. I slammed it in his face, but he managed to get through. As I had in the past, the adrenaline gave me super strength and I pushed him up against the washing machine and dryer. The impact was hard enough for him to drop Mia, who was still in his arms. 'Run bubby! Run to Nell's car!'

Mia took off and Liam and I fought violently for a while. I was copping all sorts of blows before I managed to get enough strength to shove him hard again. This time, he landed in our room with his foot going through a wall. I screamed for Maddie and Jayden to run to the car and lock the doors.

Liam got his foot free, grabbed a canvas off the wall and broke it over his knee and came at me with the broken wooden frame. The next thing I knew, his hands were so tight around my throat, it felt like he was crushing my spine. His grip was vice-like and I was powerless even as I realised he was attempting to throw me over the front second-storey balcony.

'Want to see your mum die kids? Well, she's about to!' he called out with a voice I had never heard before. It was like he had been possessed by a demon.

Hearing the commotion, my neighbour ran out of her house.

'I've called the police! Let her go!'

She was soon joined by another neighbour, who was a big, strong bloke. 'Liam, mate come on, just let her down safely. No one is mad at you. We all want to help you mate.'

His words and presence made Liam stop still and he seemed to reassess what he was doing. As he looked at me, eyes filled with unbridled hatred, he dragged me back over the railings. I fell to the floor, gasping for air as Liam started yelling out for Mia.

'Come out Bub, I'll take you to your mum's. You can't be here, it's not safe.' *The poor little thing must be so confused.* I caught a glimpse of her pink dress poking out from underneath my car and I could hear her crying for Maddie and Jayden. *She didn't get in!* Liam saw where my eyes were looking and before I could move, he dashed off down the stairs and out to the driveway, where he dragged her out from under my car.

My heart broke as I heard her screaming for me, thrashing around once more. He carried her to his Ute and literally tied her up with the seat belt before taking off with such force that his tyres spun on the concrete. I've never felt so frightened and stood frozen on the balcony watching on with hopelessness as he sped away. Even though he was gone, the tension in my throat made it feel like his hands were still choking me. I fell onto my hands and knees, rocking back as I sobbed harder than I ever had before. It was a cathartic release and it was over as quickly as it had begun. I jumped up as if hit by a lightning bolt and ran down the stairs and opened the car door to see both my children cuddled together, shaking with terror in their eyes. Seeing them like that burned me straight to my core.

'Come on let's get inside, the police will be here soon and mummy will call Uncle Michael. He'll come stay with us.'

As I walked inside, I could hear sirens as two police cars showed up. The children were sitting on the lounge watching Peppa Pig under the watchful eye of one officer while I went outside with another so we could have some privacy to talk away from the children. I guess they were directing a line of questioning to the kids too, in a roundabout way. I told the police officer everything. I remember looking at him and thinking *Wow you're really big and strong.* I hoped Liam would show up while they were there, but even if he had returned, he would've kept driving when he saw the police cars out the front.

The police gave me some instructions after the inspection of the damage to the house and collecting what information they could from me; which was a challenge as talking hurt my throat – I could hardly string a sentence together.

'Janelle, listen to us. Get all of his clothes and place them out the front. He isn't allowed to re-enter the house, we have put a call out on his number plate and we'll get him, don't worry about that.

Do you have someone that can stay with you for the next

few days?'

I told them about Michael, who was not my brother by blood but a brother in every other sense of the word. I loved Michael dearly and he always had my back. For all intents and purposes, he was family and the kids had only ever known him as Uncle Michael.

I was shaking too much to begin packing up Liam's stuff.

Jayden came up to me and placed his little hand on mine, 'Mummy, you are brave!'

The police officer just looked at Jayden and at me and he said, 'Little man, your mummy is the bravest woman I know. Now, you all look after each other and we will come over later to check on you all. We have some paperwork to do and we need to catch the bad guy.'

Jayden jumped in the air with excitement, 'YES! Get Liam, he's BAD, very BAD. He hurt my mummy.'

'Get the clothes done Janelle okay? You only have to do that right now. Go get started while we are here.'

I wasn't thinking, just doing what I was told. It was like my soul had left my body and I could no longer think. I grabbed two big bags and started putting his clothes in them. The officer explained that they weren't allowed to do it, but one sat in my room with me and the other with the children.

Once everything was packed, I did what they said and placed the bags on the driveway. I was in a complete state of fear and shock and was walking around like a zombie. The police literally had to take me through everything step by step.

'Now go inside and lock the doors. Your neighbours will keep an eye out and if he returns, they will call us straight away. Go rest with your children until Michael gets here.' I hadn't been inside for long before Michael called back. I had called him several times, which was unlike me, so he already knew something was up. When I gave him a brief rundown, he promised to pack some clothes and come over in an hour.

I settled onto the lounge holding my babies. I had tried my best to protect them from witnessing too much of the event, but I had to give them some understanding of what had happened.

'The policemen have to take Liam away. We won't see him again. He's very sick in the head and his brain isn't working properly.' It was the best I could come up with.

Jayden looked up at me and said, 'Mumma can I have an apple with the skin off please?' *Oh my sweet boy.*

'Yes buddy, come help me get it for you.'

We were standing at the kitchen bench and I still had the shakes so badly that I couldn't even peel his apple. He noticed I was struggling and said, 'Mumma I can do my own, it's okay, I'm a big strong boy.'

Just then I saw a shadow at the door. It was Liam....

Chapter 19

My Own House of Shadows

I couldn't believe what I was seeing. Here he was, back again. Within seconds he had lifted the glass sliding door out - I don't even know how he did it - and started yelling at me. Jayden placed himself between Liam and I.

'I won't let you hurt my mummy! You're a bad man!' Liam laughed in a frightening way, almost like he was possessed.

'Hahaha! You stupid little cunt, I won't just hurt your mummy, I'll hurt you and your sister too! Now fuck off!'

Something snapped in me in that moment. I felt the anger, the pain, the sadness all building in me and I was ready to explode. I picked up the biggest, sharpest knife within my reach and raised it at Liam.

'Leave now! The police are on their way back and they have all your details. Grab your shit from the front and never come back!'

As if on cue, I could hear sirens in the distance, and he ran to his car so fast and took off. His tyres screeched as he flew around the corner at the end of the street. Michael showed up shortly after, 'They got him sis. I just drove past them and they have him cornered.'

I just collapsed from pure exhaustion. Finally feeling safe with Michael in the house, I slept with the children all snuggled together.

Michael must have been up most of the night just watching out for us. I slept in and when I woke, Michael told me the police had come back around and let him know Liam was in the lockup for the night. He had been charged, but they were releasing him that day – there wasn't much more they could do until the court hearing.

'I'm moving in with you and the kids sis, you need me here. After all I'm needing a place with the messy breakup with Brooke, it all works in perfect timing as I can't stay living there with her. Kids, what do you think? Should uncle Michael move in with you guys?'

'YAY!' they cheered as they jumped up and down on the couch. 'Yes, uncle Michael!'

The police kept a close eye on me and the kids, and were in regular contact for the next few days. My bruising was really visible, and no matter how hard I tried, I couldn't cover it up. But I had to work. I had to provide for my children. There was no financial assistance to gain access to, so I went back to the salon. My staff were all super supportive and kept a close eye on me. They wouldn't allow me to even walk to the toilet by myself.

My nerves were so shot from the incident that I wasn't coping. The sound of a car beeping at the traffic lights outside my salon would startle me and send me into flight or fight mode. I couldn't even handle loud environments because I felt it dulled my ability to know what was going on around me. The police called saying Liam had been charged and pleaded guilty to all charges, but he didn't get jail time.

He was ordered to complete one hundred hours of community service, was put in a mental health program, had a two year DVO and was given a criminal record. He wasn't allowed to come anywhere near me or my children, but this is the worst part; as my salon was a public place, he couldn't be stopped from going there. He could come inside, but he couldn't talk to me or touch me. This made me so fearful because I knew he wouldn't let this go.

I would try my best to keep life as 'normal' as possible, but the sound of a broom dropping in the salon would make me jump out of my skin. The fear I felt to the depths of my core had me living life on edge, always looking over my shoulder and never feeling safe. *Where is he? How will he get revenge on me for standing up to him? How do I free myself of this nightmare? Will I ever live a life without anxiety?* I felt so trapped within my body and mind. There were days when I just wanted to scream and hide away, to forget all about the recent events. But if I allowed the darkness to take hold of me, who would look after my children? Who would look after me? The fear was so strong, but I couldn't allow it to win. I had to find a way to breathe again to break through this fog of fear.

It didn't take long for the calls to start. At first, he didn't even hide his phone number. The calls would start at strange times of the night and carry on until early morning. The voice messages increased and he was constantly driving past my salon. If he was stopped at the traffic lights outside my salon, he would run his finger across his throat and point at me. The salon phone would ring so many times with prank calls from Liam, it was as if he just wanted to hear my voice. I reported this to police and they would take my statements, talk to other witnesses and then say, 'Well, he hasn't touched you or entered the salon, so there's not really anything we can do to help you Janelle.' *Seriously? What do I have to do to be taken seriously and to get help?*

I would report breaches and keep everything I could as evidence, only to hear, 'Don't waste our time with reporting one or two breaches. Collect more, put them on a USB and then come in and we will go from there.' I ended up reporting seventy breaches in total. I had a video of him driving past my salon and making gestures that represented him wanting to cut my throat. There was this one female police officer who was present at the time of Liam's arrest and she saw me in the station one day and called out, 'Women like you are all the same. You all cry wolf and then take them back, stop. Stop wasting our time and resources!'

I looked at the officers I was sitting with at the time, unsure if I'd just heard correctly. My mouth was wide open in shock and one of them lent forward and said, 'Ignore her. She is out of line and will be dealt with. We are here to help you Janelle.' Still, I was deeply concerned that some members of the police service had that type of mindset around domestic violence. Yes, there are people out there who take the perpetrator back over and over and live that cycle. But I made the choice to be safe and I wasn't ever going back to that life. I just wanted help to be safe.

My phone was taken by police so they could strip it of any evidence they needed. It didn't feel right handing over my phone like that, but I went along with it. I was contacted a few days after this and asked if I still felt unsafe where I was living.

'Yes, I'm so scared,' I told them.

Even though Michael was still living with us, he was planning to move to the Philippines so I was really stressed about being left alone. The police suggested I check out housing that fitted a certain criteria; located on a busy road with traffic lights, close to public transport, with security sensor lights, and a high fence. *Where am I going to find a house that met all this and still be affordable?*

As fate would have it, I found one that met the requirements not long after, so I signed the lease for twelve months. I also traded in my car and got a new one so Liam would no longer know what I was driving and it would be more difficult for him to follow me. The police approved of the changes and told me to continue to report the breaches and be aware of anyone following me.

Having this cloud of fear always hanging over my head was becoming too much. I started losing so much weight and I wasn't sleeping. I was living life on repeat. I would feel safe once the gates at home were shut, but even though I had the protection of a high fence, I was still scared to have the curtains open just in case he was outside and could see me. Liam's calls started getting more intense as he couldn't locate me and he was acting out of desperation. His messages would say he needed me, he was worried about me and how much my standing up to him had made him a better man.

'I just want to know where you are and that you're okay,' he'd plead. Luckily, I was free from his spell and never faltered in keeping information from him.

New Year's Eve came around so fast that year. I spent hours

just wandering the shoreline of the beach in my local area on New Year's Day, just watching the waves roll in and being sucked back out. Something about it seemed familiar, like it was a physical manifestation of the life I'd had with Liam, and it sent a personal tidal wave through me. *Why am I equally as scared to live as I am to die?* The thought rattled me. *How did I get to this point?* As I reflected on the extremes of love and hate, light and dark, power and submission – all of the dualities that had commanded my life over the past few years – I had such a strong sense of knowing that what I had gone through should be shared. Throughout my life, I had questioned so many organisations, and shown no fear in finding the truth for me. I wanted to help other people find their own truth too.

I sat on a nearby bench to mull over this powerful insight when all of a sudden, the coldest shiver went through me. I looked over my shoulder and there he was... He was hunched over, looking unshaven and ragged and was crying, begging me to listen. The cool breeze off the ocean was nothing compared to the ice-cold feeling that shot through me in that moment. I felt like I was staring death right in the face.

'What are you doing Liam? How did you find me?'

'Just listen Nell, please just listen....'

I didn't give him a chance. I got up and ran. I ran as fast as my legs could carry me, never once looking back. I ran with an urgency befitting of the fact that my life depended on it.

When I reached my car and was safely inside with the doors locked, the honest truth is that I cried with pure sadness. I cried for what could have been and what I was running away from. I cried because the man I had loved so much had harmed me the most. I cried because his darkness would never be overcome by the light, the man I had fallen in love with.

I caught a glimpse of his face as I drove away and he looked so broken, so defeated, so lost. I cried because I could've had a part in his undoing. My love for him was what gave me the strength to fight, to gain strength to set us both free. I didn't think for a second what effect it would have on his life. All I knew was that by letting him go, I was doing what was best for the highest, greatest good.

That afternoon as I rested on my lounge reflecting on all the pain and terror of the morning, screeching tyres cut through the silence that had hung so effortlessly in the air. I sat bolt upright as this was followed by the sound of a car door being slammed and the unmistakable rumble of Liam's voice.

I instantly forgot how to breathe.

Oh my God! He's found me...

My brother wasn't there to protect me. The kids were at their dad's house. I was alone. All alone.

'NELL! I'LL GIVE YOU A CHANCE IF YOU GIVE ME ONE!'

What does he mean? Where is my phone? Oh my God, where is it? I ran through the house with my heart in my throat searching high and low for my phone so I could call for help. I was so blinded by adrenaline that I couldn't find it. Panic set in and I ran out to the shed and hid behind it. All I could hear was Liam yelling from behind the gates and banging on them incessantly.

I made myself as small as I could behind the shed and tried to keep my mind clear. *You need to focus Janelle!* The yelling and banging suddenly stopped and I waited, unsure of what to do next. After a while, I couldn't tell you how long as I'd lost all concept of time, I went back through the sliding back doors at the back of the house and caught a glimpse of his arms reaching over the top of my fence.

He is climbing over! I rushed through the doors and through blurry, tear-filled eyes, I found my phone – it was on my kitchen bench the whole time! I turned on my video and grabbed a knife on my way back outside. What I was going to do with it, I had no idea. I guess I hoped I could scare him away.

'I'm videoing you Liam. The police will get this. If you hurt me they will know, I've already messaged them.'

I had sent the alert to the private detectives and told myself it would only be moments until they arrived *I hope... oh God I hope!*

Just then, he made eye contact with me over the fence and the moment I saw his expression, I knew if he made it over before the police arrived, I'd most likely be dead. The look of hatred in his eyes was so strong that I stood frozen and lost all of the confidence I had projected just second earlier.

Then sirens echoed in the distance. I had never heard a sweeter sound in my life. Liam instantly jumped off the fence and I could hear his heavy footsteps as he ran to his car and sped off.... The police officers found me curled up on the floor, rocking in a total state of fear. I didn't even realise that they had arrived until one of them put an arm around my shoulders. When you go into such a deep fear state, it is like falling down a rabbit hole and not knowing how to get out.

When I had regained some composure, I gave my statement to the police and they took copies of all messages and video and asked me if I felt safe enough on my own. They didn't think Liam would return that night as they assumed he would've got a scare. By this stage, Liam had already gone to court a couple of times for breaches of the domestic violence court orders and he pleaded guilty to all charges. He knew if he was to face the courts again, he would more than likely face jail time. The police kept telling me they believed he wouldn't try anything stupid, but if he did, I should just contact them immediately.

As they left my house, they gave me instructions to close the curtains and keep some lights on and possibly chat to my neighbours to ask them to also keep an eye out. I was still in such a state of fear that I didn't think much of it, I simply went onto autopilot and did what I was told. Once everything was closed, locked and I'd alerted the neighbours, I went to the bathroom and ran a shower. Instead of getting in, I realised some time later that I was just sitting on the bathroom floor looking at the running water. It was as if I had disconnected from my body and gone somewhere else for those moments. *I wish I could wash all the pain and ugliness away with a simple shower.*

Chapter 20

Reaching Within

I managed to get myself settled by doing some meditation and thinking about my children and my goals in life. I knew what I had been through was for a greater reason and I just wanted to be the best version for me. I also wanted to grow my salon and live my life by example. I curled up into bed and finally managed to relax myself enough to get some sleep.

There was only the faint glow of the living room light in my doorway when I woke with a start.

BANG!

I froze.

Seconds later BANG! BANG! BANG!

I realised something was being thrown at my bedroom window. I became paralysed with fear, too afraid to move the slightest bit. There was a brief silence before there was a softer *knock, knock, knock* on my window. As if someone tapping on it with their fingers. Then came the soft, scary whisper that chilled me to the bone....

'Nell, I'm here. Nell, let me in.'

OH NOOOOOOOOO he is here! He is over the fence! I've seen him rip doors off before, what will he do now? I thought if I laid completely still and didn't make a noise, he just might think I wasn't home. I was too scared to even breathe.

'I know you're home I've been watching you. I don't want to hurt you. I just need to talk to you. I lost my daughter because of you, and I've got a criminal record. No one does that to me and I don't know why, but I still love you Nell, I need you. No one else matters, just you.'

I very quietly crawled to the bathroom and called the police. The operator asked all the usual questions; am I in danger, is someone attacking me; are they in the house... I explained that he was outside my window and not threatening me at the present time, but I was fearful for my life. The operator's response was, 'If he's not threatening to hurt you and is not physically a threat at the present time, we will put a call out to patrol but it's not a high priority job.' *What the FUCK?* I felt completely dismissed in that moment. I feared for my life and was told I was not a priority. But I didn't have time to sink energy into that feeling of abandonment at the time, I had to find a way to stall him until help arrived. *What do I do now? Just sit and wait.*

Liam started crying out for me and the pain in his voice broke my heart but I had to detach myself from it. *It's all on him, remember that.* The pain he was carrying wasn't mine to heal. I was stuck in my own nightmare of trauma and shadows from what he had done to me.

'I love you NELL!' he wailed.

How could he possibly love me? How can someone that loved me do such horrible things to me? I had lived this life and I wanted out. I wanted to free myself of this inner fear and being frozen in painful memories. *I am such a strong woman and I have overcome so much, why am I here again? What do I have to do to be free?* All these thoughts occupied my mind and I felt myself falling into darkness, so I started saying to myself, 'Janelle, you are strong, you are beautiful, you are worthy of complete happiness without living trapped in a house of shadows. Think of it like a light switch, simply flick the switch and smile, stand tall and be free.' I just kept repeating it over and over, surrendering to the moment. It was a moment that completely broke me, but at the same time, it made me.

It took about two hours before I heard police sirens…. I heard Liam gasp and leave. I just laid on the floor of the bathroom crying. Ironically, the police never came that night. The sirens we heard were headed somewhere else. Instead, I had a phone call at 4am from police asking if the disturbance was still occurring. I felt so betrayed and abandoned and when I told the officer what happened, he looked up the file and fell silent. He realised my case was much more serious than what the operator had reported and a few hours later, I was called into the police station.

When I arrived, they took me straight to the interview room and apologised for their delay in responding. They told me how understaffed they were that evening and that there were major crimes to attend to. *What a joke* I thought to myself, trying my best not to lose my cool. Their justification was that I was fine and not harmed and hopefully he wouldn't come back. They would put a call out for him and bring him in for questioning to charge him with further breaches and take him back to court.

He again pleaded guilty to all charges, but still just got a slap over the wrist. He was so good at convincing the judge that he knew the error of his ways and would stay away this time as it wasn't worth it anymore. The DV orders were extended for another year and tighter restrictions were put in place, which included my children's school, my place of work and anywhere I resided. He was also ordered to re-do a mental health rehabilitation course.

At the end of the men's Making Change Course he had to do, the psychologist contacted me saying that Liam hadn't been successful the first two times due to mental clarity. This meant he didn't meet the standards set by the course to release him from the program. The psychologist said he was very clever at trying to gaslight them, but his mental clarity wasn't present, so he would lie and then forget the details of the story he told them. He was also still classed as a flight risk.

However, upon his completion of the third course, they felt he was rehabilitated to a satisfactory degree. He was aware of the actions he had taken and was also committed to doing better, understood the consequences to his actions and was very remorseful. Liam had shown them he was trying and that did make me happy. I never wanted to cause harm to him, I just wanted him to get the help he needed. Shortly after the phone call, I received an email from Liam, it read:

> *I wanted to write this as a part of trying to let go. You taught me so much and it took losing you for me to realise a lot of things. I should have got help with depression and how to*

manage family life. You were there to help and I never saw it.

We had so many great times. I will never forget the first time I met you in Mt Isa. Our time in NZ. I will miss the bond that we have because nobody will ever be like you.

What I would do to start again. I miss our time, our cuddles, laughing with you. Most of all, I miss my best friend, being able to tell you anything and never being judged. I miss Maddie and Jayden and the bond I have with each of them.

I've lost the family that I never realised I had. My little girl has lost her brother and sister and her Nell. Mia loves you more than me, thanks for being so good to her.

I hope you find happiness with a real man who can treat you right and I wish you the best with your business and life with the kids.

What I've done will always be the biggest mistake of my life. I will always love you. Look after yourself, I will always be here for you no matter what.

Love Liam.

I didn't hear anything more from him and hope that it was all really, truly over. Each morning I woke up feeling a little safer and happier the more time passed. But the trauma I had endured remained stuck firmly within me. It's like fighting a ghost, it plays tricks with your mind and drives you to react in ways you don't even understand yourself. There was a time when I was driving along a long, straight road after dropping my children at school.

There was a roundabout approaching and to my right I saw a Ute exactly the same as Liam's. My mind went into panic and my heart raced. Instead of gripping my steering wheel, I took my hands off from the shock and was swerving off the side of the road. Luckily I realised what was happening and corrected my car before I crashed off the road. I pulled over to calm myself down only to look up and see that it wasn't Liam at all. I would put on a brave face for friends and my work colleagues, but inside I was broken. So broken.

Instead of reaching out, I reached within. I trusted myself and my intuition. I spent a lot of time in nature, I meditated, I have always been creative with colours, so my work gave me a creative outlet. I used aromatherapy, dietary therapy through a vegetarian diet, journalled my thoughts and most importantly, allowed myself to have fun, laugh and play with my children. It was my own process of recovery.

Chapter 21

Saving Me

Nearly a year had passed since I received that letter from Liam, and I met a man who I was so attracted to and slowly started a relationship with him. As the relationship progressed, I found that by opening my heart I also started releasing some deep pain I had pushed so deep, deep down. I trusted him, and by giving my trust and love, I allowed myself to be vulnerable. Our relationship lasted a couple of years but ended in him having affairs and stealing from me. You may think *why didn't I see the signs?*

The truth is, I didn't want to. I didn't want to believe that he could ever hurt me. I was so strong that I was too focused on not allowing any physical pain to happen and I opened myself to being emotionally hurt. When I found out what was going on, I didn't hesitate to end it. This time, there was no grey area. We were well and truly done. I was smarter now, I knew how it all worked.

I started to become more comfortable in being with myself and really focusing on what made me happy, but I started losing weight randomly again. My stomach just wasn't feeling right. My pain was becoming so intense around the time of my periods and I would bleed for much longer than usual. I was listening to my body and just had an intuitive thought, *This is bad and I need to take action on this quickly*. I was referred to my gynecologist for further review, taking into account my past health history. My doctor said, 'Janelle you had ovarian cancer and have been under observation for the cervical abnormalities that came back as low-grade cancerous cells, now you have had a long history with extreme endometriosis and your pain is getting worse. You have had multiple surgeries and health scares as well as having to have fertility treatment, I think your body has had enough. You're a single mother of two that need you and if we don't preform a hysterectomy, the next stage isn't going to be a pleasant one.'

She said if I didn't remove the cancer and the organs affected there was a strong possibility the cancer would rapidly turn worse, so I decided to fight. Fight for the freedom of my soul, my heart, and my mind. So, I had the major surgery, removing six organs and starting treatment to help with a successful recovery. My support team was made up of five of my closest friends. Not having a partner or family to turn to was not a problem at all; I was so happy and completely supported with the family I chose for myself.

Call it an inner knowing, but a pathway for my future self to be able to stand up and make a difference for all started to become clear. I was getting up every day during my recovery to a message from my soul sister Livia. She always listened to me and was always up for an adventure, but when the cards were down she was the first by my side. During my life I have been blessed with the right people for the right reasons and Livia called me one morning while I was out on my walk, the same walk I did daily, with a clear message for me.

'Janelle I've seen you get knocked down more times than anyone and you always get back up. After your car accident I visited you when you didn't think you'd ever be able to pick your children up again or even hold a cup of coffee. Remember, I said to you then, you could've lost your arms and legs and it wouldn't have changed you. You still would be living life and being happy because that's who you are. Don't let this operation break you, let it make you. I believe in you! Now get better and then make this messed up world a better place. I know you will, it's your destiny. You haven't gone through all the bullshit not to help others. I LOVE YOU.'

With that, it was decided. I made my mind up to heal myself and help others. How I was going to do this was such an unknown, but I just kept doing the work on myself and trusted the path would become clear. I allowed love in. I gave love as well.

I dated, but just didn't find anyone that was on my level. They were either too controlling, or they were too disconnected, and just didn't have the drive for life I was looking for. I heard it all; 'Janelle you're too busy, you aren't available when I want you.'

'You don't need me and that is intimidating for a man.'

'You should make more time for me....'

It was all, 'I want, I want, I want, I need, I need, I need.' I just couldn't believe that my experience was finding men who said they loved the idea of a strong, independent woman, but really only wanted a needy female. When they would come out with ways I should need them more, I would remind them of that.

'Hang on, when we started dating, the fact I had worked out who I am and that I am driven, successful, positive and ready to just enjoy life was what you said you wanted!'

The responses I received were so closed-minded and selfish. They either wanted me to abandon my dreams and settle down to be at their side supporting their goals, or they wanted a free ride with me.

So I started again asking myself, *What is it that I want? What will make my life better? How do I grow from this and recognise within myself what is holding me back from really feeling safe with a man?*

What I realised was it wasn't just love and relationships with men, it was love itself that I needed to redefine. I grew up learning that pain equalled love. That when you trust someone who says that they won't hurt you, they would. That hurt could come in all sorts of forms from physical violence and verbal abuse to cheating and stealing. I had experienced all of it.

My life was a complicated mixture of fear, happiness, distrust, joy, darkness, control and a desire for something better, something magical.

To be able to face your own truth you have to be brave - braver than you ever thought possible. Because standing in front of yourself in a mirror and realising your patterns and truly seeing yourself and all the scars you've collected from your pain – the ones that no one else sees, knows about or even believes – is where it all starts.

To do this allows you to not just escape your house of shadows – but to blow up everything that was – in order to accept your own truth without fear, shame, blame and guilt. Once you do that, you can rebuild your own palace of love, kindness, playfulness, adventures and happiness from the rubble.

I've learned not to put limiting stereotype beliefs on myself and others. From growing up in a house of shadows with twists and turns, the emotions that grow inside you create fear that causes distrust, lack of self-worth and harsh judgments. Through my healing from a trauma state, I have healed the addiction to the adrenaline feeling you get from a release of the stress hormones. It's like a drug; you know it's not good for you, you want to escape the control it has on you, but it's a cycle that you are taught, and breaking that takes work. Taking responsibility for your own pain, for your own shame, blame, guilt and unworthiness and starting to show yourself forgiveness, love and self-worth is how you work through it.

We need to take a step back and ask ourselves why? That question is simple, but also the hardest to ask. Trust me, I know how hard it is, but when we face the facts and be brave, we can allow ourselves to be lost and to rise again fearless and renewed.

Violence is never okay on any level. Physical, sexual, psychological, verbal, emotional, financial and spiritual abuse is not okay. I have done the work to recognise my role in my past and I have found the beauty of allowing myself to forgive the pain I held in my heart. I can also acknowledge that those who hurt me were also hurting. I am not saying you have to have these dangerous people in your life and I am not saying forgiveness is something you have to do face to face.

I've seen the beauty of my soul, the strength of my mind, and the ability to heal my heart to release myself from the past and gain the beauty of life that unfolds each and every day. I learnt that we all hurt, and the people that cause pain to us are usually hurting so deeply themselves. It is not your responsibility or mine to hurt them back, it is not our right to cause pain directly to someone else. All we can do is hold our truth and stand up for it. By doing so, the consequences of their acts of terror will be dealt with by the universe. Acts of violence towards anyone on any level is not okay, and two wrongs do not make a right. By telling your story and learning from each other, we can all free ourselves from our own house of shadows.

Forgive yourself. Love yourself. Be proud that you have the power and ability within you to escape your house of shadows. One day you will see again, breathe again, and love yourself.

Love, Janelle.

Acknowledgements

This book is the result of a lifetime of work and a journey of six years to get it all down on these pages.

I am very blessed and thankful for the love and support of my children Maddie and Jayden. We have moved far beyond the shadows and continue to grow together in a life full of light.

To my Poppy and soul brother Michael Farrow, I miss you both more than words can say. Your protection and support mean the world to me and gave me hope in some of my darkest moments. Rest in peace.

To my loving Nanna, my soul sister Livia Simpson, my Meek HD team and my dear friends who are also my family – you know who you are. Your encouragement to stand tall and tell my story were the fuel that kept me going throughout the process of writing this book. Thank you for all of the fun, goofy times and equally for being there in times when I needed a hug.

About the Author

Janelle Parsons is a mother, author, businesswoman, domestic violence spokeswoman and the founder of House of No Shadows.

She credits reaching a place of unconditional love for herself as being the beacon of light on her path to happiness, ultimately giving her the ability to accept and forgive herself and others. She now empowers others to do the same.

Janelle has a way of bringing attention to the things that may have been buried for so long, things you never knew were there. Her process is calm and concise, so you can be guided to release old ways that don't serve you, so you will be free to move forward and heal your pain.

Janelle's framework comes from her great depth of understanding of the heartache that comes from childhood and adult trauma. Having overcome her own house of shadows, Janelle knows how to shine a light on even the toughest topics and helps lift you out of darkness.

She does things very much outside the box and pushes the boundaries to get the best results for her clients – all while having fun of course!

To find out more, visit *www.janelleparsons.com*

With so many secretly suffering....

On the website, you'll find resources you can access with ease, courses that will elevate you beyond your experiences and into new choices driven by freedom rather than escaping a painful past.

Access to podcasts, interviews and blogs.

If you found these pages enlightening, informative or educational, I'd love to join you online at:

www.janelleparsons.com

JANELLE PARSONS
PUBLISHING

www.ingramcontent.com/pod-product-compliance
Lightning Source LLC
Chambersburg PA
CBHW030254010526
44107CB00053B/1710